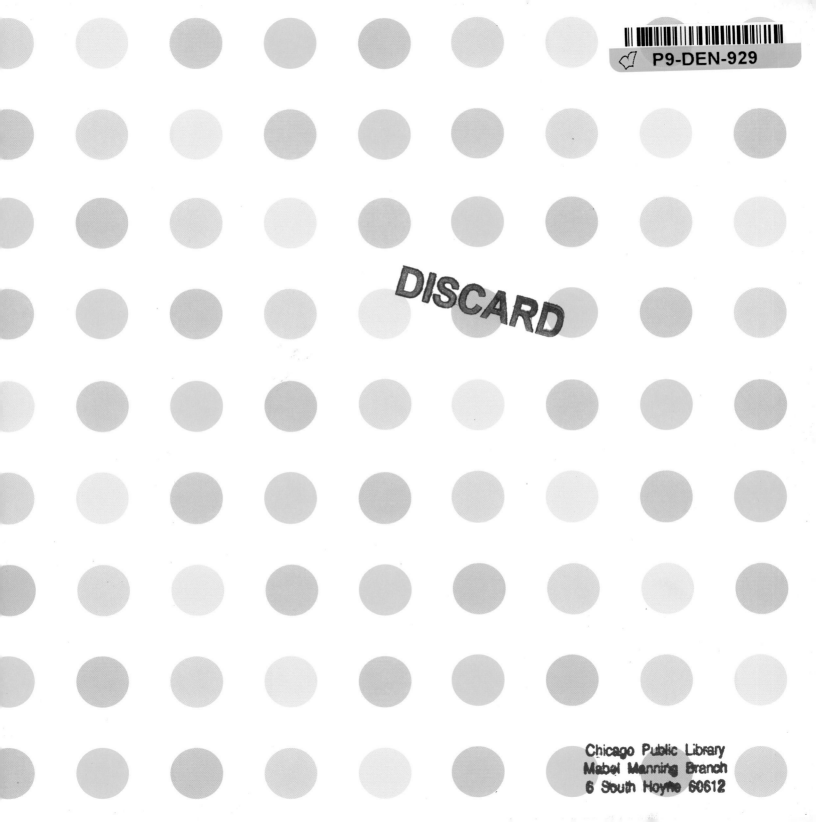

DISCARD

P9-DEN-929

ESSENTIAL baby

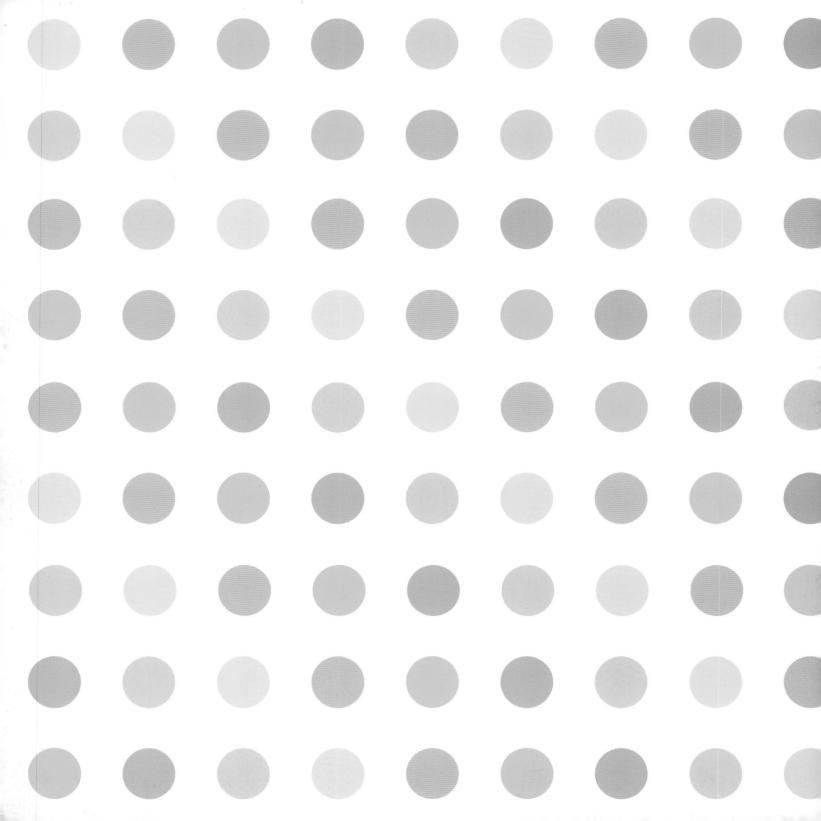

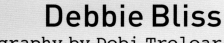

Debbie Bliss

photography by Debi Treloar

ESSENTIAL baby

over 20 hand knits to take your baby from
first days to first steps

Trafalgar Square Books
North Pomfret, Vermont

4

First published in the United States of America in 2007
by **Trafalgar Square Books**
North Pomfret, Vermont 05053.

Printed in Singapore

Originally published in the United Kingdom in 2007 by
Quadrille Publishing Limited, London.

Text and project designs
© 2007 Debbie Bliss
Photography, design, and layout
© 2007 Quadrille Publishing Limited

Library of Congress Control Number: 2006911308

ISBN: 978-1-57076-368-7

Editorial Director **Jane O'Shea**
Creative Director **Mary Evans**
Project Editor **Lisa Pendreigh**
Editorial Assistant **Andrew Bayliss**
Photographer **Debi Treloar**
Stylist **Julie Mansfield**
Techniques Illustrator **Kate Simunek**
Pattern Illustrator **Bridget Bodoano**
Production Director **Vincent Smith**
Production Controller **Ruth Deary**

10 9 8 7 6 5 4 3 2 1

First edition

introduction

The period immediately before the arrival of a baby is a unique time for nesting, perfect for creating special hand knits to welcome a newborn infant home. With this in mind, in **Essential Baby** I have designed a capsule collection to take a baby through from his or her first few days to their first few steps.

Divided into three sections—Coming Home, At Home, and On the Go—this book provides every new parent with the key knitted pieces needed for baby's first eighteen months.

Coming Home is full of baby must-haves: a snuggle-into shawl, a hooded carrying bag in a cashmere mix—gentle against a baby's delicate skin—while a simple crossover top,

pants, and coat provide a contemporary feel to the classic layette. As well as everything you need to wrap up your precious little one and keep them cozy, to welcome your baby home there are projects such as a knitted house picture and a cuddly toy lamb for baby's first room.

At Home is for downtime, with a cozy cotton bathrobe—a great wraparound for after a bath—and slip-on felted slippers. Soft vintage-style knee-length shorts and romper panties are both perfect for crawlers, while for playtime there is a squashy beanbag for baby to relax and kick back on and a heart mobile to hang over the crib.

On the Go includes outdoor basics that will keep your baby snug on trips

out and about: a practical changing mat that doubles as a carrying bag, a double-sided patchwork and striped blanket to tuck around baby in the stroller, a reversible hat, chunky cable-knit socks, and a double-breasted duffle coat.

All the yarns from my ranges have been especially chosen for comfort and practicality. There are cashmere mixes, extra-fine merino wools, and classic cottons, which are all machine washable but at the same time are soft and gentle against young skin.

I have designed the projects to cover a range of knitting skills, but most are simple, reflecting a new life balance when nurturing may take over from knitting.

knitting basics

types of yarns

When choosing a yarn for babies or children, it is essential that you work with a fiber that is soft and gentle against a baby's skin. Babies are not able to tell you if a collar is rough against their neck or if cuffs are irritating their wrists, and as older children are often more used to the lightweight freedom of fleeces, they can be resistant to hand knits that they may consider scratchy and uncomfortable.

The yarns I have chosen for this book are cashmere combined with merino wool (giving softness and durability), pure cotton, and extra-fine merino. Although they create fabrics that are soft to wear, most importantly all these yarns are machine washable.

Wherever possible try to buy the yarn specified in the pattern. All these designs have been created with a specific yarn in mind: the Shawl Collar Sweater is worked in a soft yarn to gently frame a baby's face, while the Changing Mat Bag is made in a natural cotton to give it the necessary sturdiness to maintain its shape—a floppier fiber or a synthetic yarn would create a limp fabric. From an aesthetic point of view, the clarity of a subtle stitch pattern may be lost if a garment is knitted in an inferior yarn.

There may be occasions when a knitter needs to substitute a yarn—if the wearer has an allergy to wool, for example—and so the following is a guideline to making the most informed choices.

Always buy a yarn that is the same weight as that given in the pattern, and check that the recommended gauge of both yarns is the same.

Where you are substituting a different fiber, be aware of the design. A cable pattern knitted in cotton when worked in wool will pull in because of the greater elasticity of the yarn and so the fabric will become narrower; this will alter the proportions of the garment.

Check the yardage of the yarn. Yarns that weigh the same may have different lengths of ball or hank, so you may need to buy more or less yarn.

Here are descriptions of my yarns and a guide to their weights and types:

Debbie Bliss alpaca silk aran:
80% alpaca, 20% silk.
Approximately 71yd (1³/₄oz/50g) per ball.
Debbie Bliss caby cashmerino:
55% merino wool, 33% microfiber,
12% cashmere.
Approximately 137yd (1³/₄oz/50g) per ball.
Debbie Bliss cashmerino aran:
55% merino wool, 33% microfiber,
12% cashmere.
Approximately 99yd (1³/₄oz/50g) per ball.
Debbie Bliss cashmerino astrakhan:
60% merino wool, 30% microfiber,
10% cashmere.
Approximately 77yd (1³/₄oz/50g) per ball.
Debbie Bliss cashmerino double knitting:
55% merino wool, 33% microfiber,
12% cashmere.

Approximately 120yd (1³/₄oz/50g) per ball.
Debbie Bliss cotton double knitting:
100% cotton.
Approximately 92yd (1³/₄oz/50g) ball.
Debbie Bliss rialto double knitting:
100% extra-fine merino wool.
Approximately 115yd (1³/₄oz/50g) ball.

buying yarn

The yarn label will carry all the essential information you need as to gauge, needle size, weight, and yardage. Importantly, it will also have the dye lot number. Yarns are dyed in batches or lots, which can vary considerably. As your retailer may not have the same dye lot later on, buy all your yarn for a project at the same time. If you know that sometimes you use more yarn than that quoted in the pattern, buy extra. If it is not possible to buy all the yarn you need with the same dye lot, use the different ones where it will not show as much, on a neck or border, as a change of dye lot across a main piece will most likely show.

It is also a good idea at the time of buying the yarn that you check the pattern and make sure that you already have the needles you will require. If not, buy them now because it will save a lot of frustration when you get home.

garment care

Taking care of your hand knits is important because you want them to look good for as long as possible. Correct washing is particularly important for baby garments because they need to be washed frequently.

Check the yarn label for washing instructions to see whether the yarn is hand or machine washable, and if it is the latter, at what temperature it should be washed.

Most hand knits should be dried flat on an absorbent cloth, such as a towel, to soak up any moisture. Lying them flat in this way gives you an opportunity to pat the garment back into shape if it has become pulled around in the washing machine. Even if you are in a hurry, do not be tempted to dry your knits near a direct heat source, such as a radiator.

As baby garments are small, you may prefer to hand wash them. Use a washing agent that is specifically designed for knitwear since this will be kinder to the fabric. Use warm rather than hot water and handle the garment gently without rubbing or wringing. Let the water out of the sink and then gently squeeze out the excess water. Do not lift out a water-logged knit as the weight of the water will pull it out of shape. You may need to remove more moisture by rolling it in a towel. Dry flat as explained for machine washing.

techniques

cast on

slip knot

Your first step when beginning to knit is to work a foundation row called a cast-on. Without this row you cannot begin to knit.

There are several methods of casting on. You can choose a method to serve a particular purpose or because you feel comfortable with that particular technique. The two examples shown here are the ones I have found to be the most popular, the thumb and the cable methods.

In order to work a cast-on edge, you must first make a slip knot.

1 Wind the yarn around the fingers on your left hand to make a circle of yarn as shown above. With the knitting needle, pull a loop of the yarn attached to the ball through the yarn circle on your fingers.

2 Pull both ends of the yarn to tighten the slip knot on the knitting needle. You are now ready to begin, using either of the following cast-on techniques.

cast on

thumb cast-on

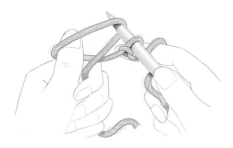

1 Make a slip knot as shown on page 15, leaving a long tail end. With the slip knot on the needle in your right hand and the yarn that comes from the ball over your index finger, wrap the tail end of the yarn over your left thumb from front to back, holding the yarn in your palm with your fingers.

2 Insert the knitting needle upward through the yarn loop on your left thumb.

The thumb cast-on is a one needle method that produces a flexible edge, which makes it particularly useful for nonelastic yarns such as cotton. The "give" in it also makes it a good cast-on to use where the edge will turn back, as on the Duffle Coat (see page 130).

Unlike two-needle methods you are working toward the yarn end, which means you have to predict the length you need to cast on the required number of stitches, otherwise you may find you do not have enough yarn to complete the last few stitches and have to start all over again. If unsure, always allow for more yarn than you think you need because you can use what is left over for sewing seams.

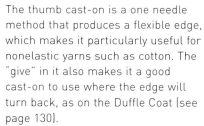

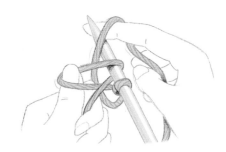

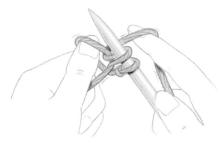

3 With the right index finger, wrap the yarn from the ball up and over the tip of the knitting needle.

4 Draw the yarn through the loop on your thumb to form a new stitch on the knitting needle. Then, let the yarn loop slip off your left thumb and pull the loose end to tighten up the stitch. Repeat these steps until the required number of stitches have been cast on.

cable cast-on

1 Make a slip knot as shown on page 15. Hold the knitting needle with the slip knot in your left hand and insert the right-hand needle from left to right and from front to back through the slip knot. Wrap the yarn from the ball up and over the tip of the right-hand needle as shown.

2 With the right-hand needle, draw a loop through the slip knot to make a new stitch. Do not drop the stitch from the left-hand needle, but instead slip the new stitch onto the left-hand needle as shown.

The cable cast-on method uses two needles and is particularly good for ribbed edges, as it provides a sturdy, but still elastic, edge. Because you need to insert the needle between the stitches and pull the yarn through to create another stitch, make sure that you do not make the new stitch too tight. The cable method is one of the most widely used cast-ons.

3 Next, insert the right-hand needle between the two stitches on the left-hand needle and wrap the yarn around the tip of the right-hand needle.

4 Pull the yarn through to make a new stitch, and then place the new stitch on the left-hand needle, as before. Repeat the last two steps until the required number of stitches have been cast on.

knit

The knit and purl stitches form the basis of almost all knitted fabrics. The knit stitch is the easiest to learn and is the first stitch you will create. When worked continuously it forms a reversible fabric called garter stitch. You can recognize garter stitch by the horizontal ridges formed at the top of the knitted loops.

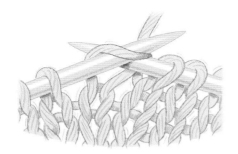

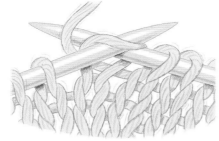

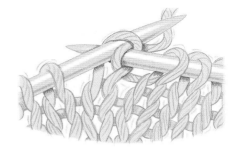

1 With the cast-on stitches on the needle in your left hand, insert the right-hand needle from left to right and from front to back through the first cast-on stitch.

2 Take the yarn from the ball on your index finger (the working yarn) around the tip of the right-hand needle.

3 Draw the right-hand needle and yarn through the stitch, thus forming a new stitch on the right-hand needle, and at the same time slip the original stitch off the left-hand needle. Repeat these steps until all the stitches from the left-hand needle have been worked. One knit row has now been completed.

&purl

After the knit stitch you should learn the purl stitch. If the purl stitch is worked continuously, it forms the same fabric as garter stitch. However, if purl rows and knit rows are worked alternately, they create stockinette stitch, which is the most widely used knitted fabric.

1 With the yarn to the front of the work, insert the right-hand needle from the right to the left into the front of the first stitch on the left-hand needle.

2 Then take the yarn from the ball on your index finger (the working yarn) around the tip of the right-hand needle.

3 Draw the right-hand needle and the yarn through the stitch, thus forming a new stitch on the right-hand needle, and at the same time slip the original stitch off the left-hand needle. Repeat these steps until all the stitches have been worked. One purl row has now been completed.

increase

increase one

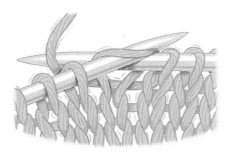 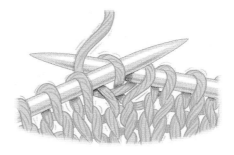

1 Insert the right-hand needle into the front of the next stitch, then knit the stitch but leave it on the left-hand needle.

2 Insert the right-hand needle into the back of the same stitch and knit it. Then slip the original stitch off the needle. Now you have made an extra stitch on the right-hand needle.

make one

Increases are used to add to the width of the knitted fabric by creating more stitches. They are worked, for example, when shaping sleeves up the length of the arm or when additional stitches are needed after a ribbed border. Some increases are invisible, while others are worked away from the edge of the work and are meant to be seen in order to give decorative detail. Most knitting patterns will tell you which type of increase to make.

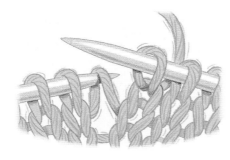 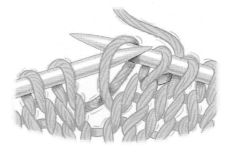

1 Insert the left-hand needle from front to back under the horizontal strand between the stitch just worked on the right-hand needle and the first stitch on the left-hand needle.

2 Knit into the back of the loop to twist it, and to prevent a hole. Drop the strand from the left-hand needle. This forms a new stitch on the right-hand needle.

yarn over

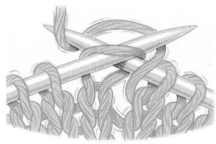

yarn over between knit stitches
Bring the yarn forward between the two needles, from the back to the front of the work. Taking the yarn over the right-hand needle to do so, knit the next stitch.

yarn over between purl stitches
Bring the yarn over the right-hand needle to the back, then between the two needles to the front. Then purl the next stitch.

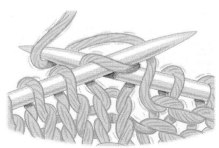

yarn over between a purl and a knit
Take the yarn from the front over the right-hand needle to the back. Then knit the next stitch.

yarn over between a knit and a purl
Bring the yarn forward between the two needles from the back to the front of the work, and take it over the top of the right-hand needle to the back again and then forward between the needles. Then purl the next stitch.

bindoff

knit bind-off

1 Knit two stitches. Insert the left-hand needle into the first stitch knitted on the right-hand needle and lift this stitch over the second stitch and off the right-hand needle.

2 One stitch is now on the right-hand needle. Knit the next stitch. Repeat the first step until all the stitches have been bound off. Pull the yarn through the last stitch to fasten off.

purl bind-off

Binding off is used to finish off your knitted piece so that the stitches don't unravel. It is also used to decrease more than one stitch at a time, such as when shaping armholes, neckbands, and buttonholes. It is important that a bind-off is firm but elastic, particularly when you are binding off around a neckband, to ensure that it can be pulled easily over the head. Unless told otherwise, bind off in the pattern stitch used in the piece.

1 Purl two stitches. Insert the left-hand needle into the back of the first stitch worked on the right-hand needle and lift this stitch over the second stitch and off the right-hand needle.

2 One stitch is now on the right-hand needle. Purl the next stitch. Repeat the first step until all the stitches have been bound off. Pull the yarn through the last stitch to fasten off.

decrease

knit 2 together

knit 2 together ("k2tog" or "dec one")
On a knit row, insert the right-hand needle from left to right through the next two stitches on the left-hand needle and knit them together. One stitch has been decreased.

purl 2 together

purl 2 together ("p2tog" or "dec one")
On a purl row, insert the right-hand needle from right to left through the next two stitches on the left-hand needle. Then purl them together. One stitch has been decreased.

slip stitch over

Decreases are used to make the fabric narrower by getting rid of stitches on the needle. They are worked to make an opening for a neckline or shaping a sleeve cap. As with increases, they can be used to create decorative detail, often around a neck edge. Increases and decreases are used together to create lace patterns.

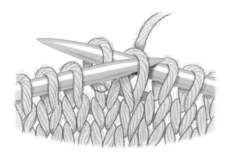

slip 1, knit 1, pass slipped stitch over ("skp")
1 Insert the right-hand needle into the next stitch on the left-hand needle and slip it onto the right-hand needle without knitting it. Knit the next stitch. Then insert the left-hand needle into the slipped stitch as shown.

2 With the left-hand needle, lift the slipped stitch over the knitted stitch as shown, and off the right-hand needle.

reading patterns

To those unfamiliar with knitting patterns they can appear to be written in a strange, alien language! However, as you become used to the terminology you will see that they have a logic and consistency that you will soon become familiar with.

Do not be too concerned if you read through a pattern first and are confused by parts of it because some instructions make more sense when your stitches are on the needle and you are at that stage in the knitting. However, it is sometimes a good idea to check with your yarn store whether your skill levels are up to a particular design to prevent frustration later on.

Figures for larger sizes are given in parentheses ( ). Where only one figure appears, it means that this number applies to all sizes. Directions in brackets [ ] should be repeated as many times as instructed. Where 0 (zero) appears, no stitches or rows are worked for this size.

When you follow the pattern, it is important that you consistently use the right stitches or rows for the size. Switching between sizes can be avoided by marking your size throughout with a highlighting pen on a photocopy of the pattern.

Before starting your project, check the size and the actual measurements that are quoted for that size; you may want to make a smaller or larger garment depending on the proportions of the wearer it is intended for.

The quantities of yarn given in the instructions are based on the yarn used by the knitter of the original garment, and therefore all amounts should be considered approximate.

For example, if that knitter has used almost all of the last ball, it may be that another knitter with a slightly different gauge has to start another ball to complete the garment. A slight variation in gauge can therefore make the difference between using fewer or more balls than stated in the pattern.

gauge

Every knitting pattern gives a gauge—the number of stitches and rows to 4 inches that should be obtained with the specified yarn, needle size, and stitch pattern. It is essential to check your gauge before starting your project. A slight variation can alter the proportions of the finished garment and the look of the fabric. A gauge that is too loose will produce an uneven and unstable fabric that can drop or lose its shape after washing, while one that is too tight can create a hard, inelastic fabric.

Making a gauge square
Use the same needles, yarn, and stitch pattern quoted in the gauge note in the pattern. Knit a sample at least 5 inches square to get the most accurate result. Smooth out the finished sample on a

flat surface, making sure you are not stretching it out.

To check the stitch gauge, place a tape measure or ruler horizontally on the sample and mark 4 inches with pins. Count the number of stitches between the pins. To check the row gauge, mark 4 inches with pins vertically and count the number of rows. If the number of stitches and rows is greater than specified in the pattern, your gauge is tighter and you should change to a larger needle size and make another gauge square. If there are fewer stitches and rows, your gauge is looser and you should try again on a smaller needle size. The stitch gauge is the most important to get right, since the number of stitches in a pattern is set but the length is given as a measurement rather than in rows, and you may be able to work more or fewer rows.

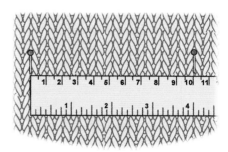

abbreviations

The following are the general abbreviations used throughout this book. If any special abbreviations are needed, they are provided at the beginning of the individual patterns.

standard abbreviations

alt = alternate
beg = begin(ning)
cont = continu(e)(ing)
dec = decreas(e)(ing)
foll = follow(s)(ing)
inc = increas(e)(ing)
k = knit
M1 = make one stitch by picking up the loop lying between the stitch just worked and the next stitch and working into the back of it
patt = pattern; or work in pattern
p = purl
psso = pass slipped stitch over
rem = remain(s)(ing)
rep = repeat(s)(ing)
rev St st = reverse stockinette stitch
skp = slip 1, knit 1, pass slipped stitch over
sl = slip
st(s) = stitch(es)
St st = stockinette stitch
tbl = through back of loop
tog = together
yo = yarn over right-hand needle to make a new stitch

cables

back cross cable

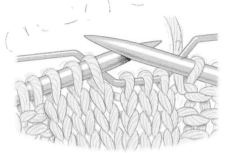 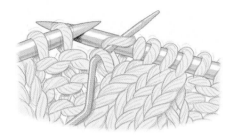

1 Slip the first three cable stitches purlwise off the left-hand needle and onto the cable needle. Leave the cable needle at the back of the work, then knit the next three stitches on the left-hand needle, keeping the yarn tight to prevent a gap from forming in the knitting.

2 Knit the three stitches directly from the cable needle, or if preferred, slip the three stitches from the cable needle back onto the left-hand needle and then knit them. This completes the cable cross.

front cross cable

Cables are formed by the simple technique of crossing one set of stitches over another. Stitches are held on a cable needle (a short double-pointed needle) at the back or front of the work while the same amount of stitches is worked from the left-hand needle. Simple cables form a vertical twisted rope of stockinette stitch on a background of reverse stockinette stitch and tend to be worked over four or six stitches.

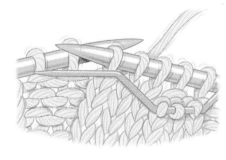 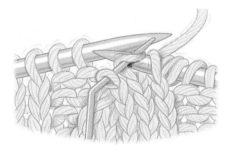

1 Slip the first three cable stitches purlwise off the left-hand needle and onto the cable needle. Leave the cable needle at the front of the work, then knit the next three stitches on the left-hand needle, keeping the yarn tight to prevent a gap from forming in the knitting.

2 Knit the three stitches directly from the cable needle, or if preferred, slip the three stitches from the cable needle back onto the left-hand needle and then knit them. This completes the cable cross.

intarsia

Intarsia is used when you are working with larger areas of usually isolated color, such as when knitting large motifs. If the yarn not in use were stranded or woven into the wrong side, it could show through to the front or pull in the colorwork. In intarsia you use a separate strand or small ball of yarn for each color area and then twist the colors together where they meet to prevent a gap forming.

vertical

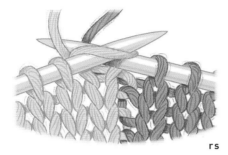

rs

ws

right diagonal

rs

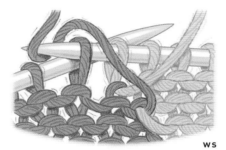

ws

left diagonal

rs

ws

changing colors on a vertical line
If the two color areas are forming a vertical line, to change colors on a knit row drop the color you were using. Pick up the new color and wrap it around the dropped color as shown, then continue with the new color. Twist the yarns together on knit and purl rows in this same way at vertical-line color changes.

changing colors on a right diagonal
If the two color areas are forming a right diagonal line, on a knit row drop the color you were using. Pick up the new color and wrap it around the dropped color as shown, then continue with the new color. Twist the yarns together on knit rows only at right-diagonal color changes.

changing colors on a left diagonal
If the two color areas are forming a left diagonal line, on a purl row drop the color you were using. Pick up the new color and wrap it around the color just dropped as shown, then continue with the new color. Twist the yarns together on purl rows only at left-diagonal color changes.

reading charts

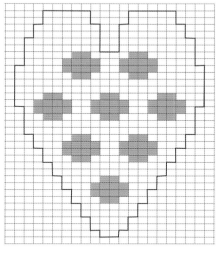

☐ A ecru   ▨ C lime

Most color patterns are worked from a chart rather than set out in the text. Each square represents a stitch and row and the symbol or color within it will tell you which color to use. There will be a key listing the symbols used and the colors they represent.

Unless stated otherwise, the first row of the chart is worked from right to left and represents the first right-side row of your knitting. The second chart row represents the second and wrong-side row and is read and worked from left to right.

If the color pattern is a repeated design, as in Fair Isle, the chart will tell you how many stitches are in each repeat. You will repeat these stitches

as many times as is required. At each side of the repeat there may be edge stitches, these are only worked at the beginning and end of the rows and they indicate where you need to start and end for the piece you are knitting. Most color patterns are worked in stockinette stitch.

stranding

stranding on a knit row

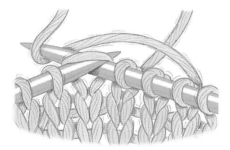

1 On a right-side (knit) row, to change colors drop the color you were using. Pick up the new color, take it over the top of the dropped color and start knitting with it.

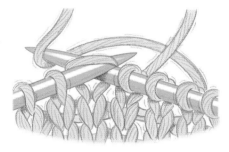

2 To change back to the old color, drop the color you were knitting with. Pick up the old color, take it under the dropped color and knit to the next color change, and so on.

stranding on a purl row

Stranding is used when each of two colors is worked over a small number of stitches. The color you are not using is left hanging on the wrong side of the work and is then picked up when it is needed again. This creates strands at the back of the work called floats. Care must be taken not to pull the floats too tightly as this will pucker the fabric. By picking up the yarns over and under one another you will prevent them from tangling.

1 On a wrong-side (purl) row, to change colors drop the color you were using. Pick up the new color, take it over the top of the dropped color and start purling with it.

2 To change back to the old color, drop the color you were knitting with. Pick up the old color, take it under the dropped color and purl to the next color change, and so on.

seams

When you have completed the pieces of your knitting, you reach one of the most important stages. The way you finish your project determines how good the finished garment will look. There are different seam techniques, but the best by far is mattress or ladder stitch, which creates an invisible seam. It can be used on ribbing, stockinette stitch, garter stitch, and seed stitch.

The seam that I use for almost all seams is mattress stitch, which produces a wonderful invisible seam. It works well in any yarn, and makes a completely straight seam, as the same amount is taken up on each side—this also means that the knitted pieces should not need to be pinned together first. It is always worked on the right side of the fabric and is particularly useful for sewing seams on stripes and Fair Isle.

I use other types of seams less frequently, but they do have their uses. For instance, backstitch can sometimes be useful for sewing in a sleeve cap, to neatly ease in the fullness. It is also good for catching in loose strands of

yarn on colorwork seams, where there can be a lot of short ends along the selvage. Just remember when using backstitch for seams on your knitting that it is important to ensure that you work in a completely straight line.

The seam for joining two bound-off edges is handy for shoulder seams, while the seam for joining a bound-off edge with a side edge (selvage) is usually used when sewing a sleeve to the body on a dropped shoulder style.

It is best to leave a long tail end at the casting-on stage to use for seams, so that the seaming yarn is already secured in place. If this is not possible, when first securing the yarn for the seam, leave a length that can be darned

in afterward. All seams on knitting should be sewn with a large blunt-ended yarn or tapestry needle to avoid splitting the yarn.

Before sewing side seams, sew the shoulder seams and attach the sleeves, unless they are set in sleeves. If there are any embellishments, such as applied pockets or embroidery, this is the time to put them on, when you can lay the garment out flat.

seams

mattress stitch on stockinette stitch and double ribbing
With the right sides of the knitting facing you, insert the needle under the horizontal bar between the first stitch and next stitch. Then insert the needle under the same bar on the other piece. Continue to do this, pulling through the yarn to form the seam.

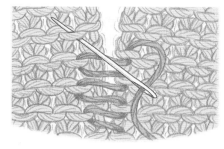

mattress stitch on garter stitch
With the right sides of the knitting facing you, insert the needle through the bottom of the "knot" on the edge and then through the top of the corresponding "knot" on the opposite edge. Continue to do this from edge to edge, pulling through the yarn to form a flat seam.

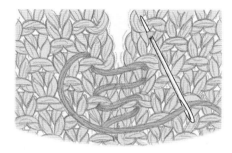

mattress stitch on seed stitch
With the right sides of the knitting facing you, insert the needle under the horizontal bar between the first and second stitches on one side and through the top of the "knot" on the edge of the opposite side.

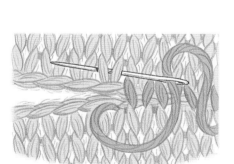

joining two bound-off edges (grafting)
1 With the bound-off edges butted together, bring the needle out in the center of the first stitch just below the bound-off edge on one piece. Insert the needle through the center of the first stitch on the other piece and out through the center of the next stitch.

2 Next, insert the needle through the center of the first stitch on the first piece again and out through the center of the stitch next to it. Continue in this way until the seam is completed.

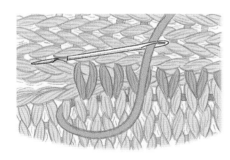

joining bound-off and selvage edges
Bring the needle from back to front through the center of the first stitch on the bound-off edge. Then insert it under one or two horizontal strands between the first and second stitches on the selvage and back through the center of the same bound-off stitch. Continue in this way.

pickingupstitches

When you are adding a border to your garment, such as front bands or a neckband, you usually pick up stitches around the edge. A border can be sewn on afterward but this method is far neater. If you are picking up stitches along a long edge, a front band of a jacket for example, a long circular needle can be used so that you can fit all the stitches on. The pattern will usually tell you how many stitches to pick up.

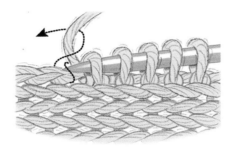

picking up stitches along a selvage
With the right side of the knitting facing, insert the knitting needle from front to back between the first and second stitches of the first row. Wrap the yarn around the needle and pull a loop through to a form a new stitch on the needle. Continue in this way along the edge of the knitting.

picking up stitches along a neck edge
On a neck edge, work along the straight edges as for a selvage. But along the curved edges, insert the needle through the center of the stitch below the shaping (to avoid large gaps) and pull a loop of yarn through to form a new stitch on the needle.

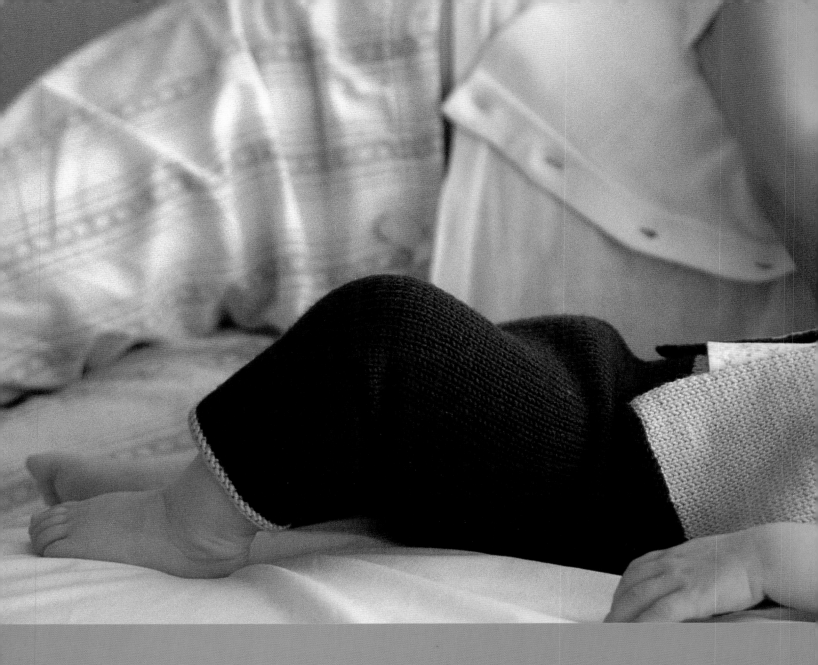

coming home

crossover top

sizes and measurements
To fit ages 0–3 (3–6: 6–9: 9–12) months
finished measurements
Chest 16$\frac{1}{2}$ (18: 19$\frac{3}{4}$: 21$\frac{1}{4}$)in
Length to shoulder 10$\frac{1}{4}$ (11: 11$\frac{3}{4}$: 12$\frac{1}{2}$)in
Sleeve length 4$\frac{3}{4}$ (5: 5$\frac{1}{2}$: 6$\frac{1}{4}$)in

materials
2 (3: 3: 3) x 1$\frac{3}{4}$oz/50g balls Debbie Bliss Baby Cashmerino in lilac (M) and a small amount in chocolate (C)
Pair each of sizes 2 and 3 knitting needles
24in of ribbon, $\frac{1}{4}$in wide
One small button

gauge
25 sts and 34 rows to 4in square over St st using size 3 needles.

abbreviations
See page 25.

back

With size 2 needles and C, cast on 65 (70: 75: 80) sts.
K 1 row.
Change to size 3 needles and M.
Beg with a k row, work in St st.
Work 6 (8: 10: 10) rows.
Dec row (right side) K8, skp, k to last 10 sts, k2tog, k8.
Work 9 (9: 9: 11) rows.
Rep the last 10 (10: 10: 12) rows 3 times more and the dec row again. **55 (60: 65: 70) sts.**
Work even until back measures 6³/₄ (7: 8: 8¹/₄)in from cast-on edge, ending with a p row.
Shape armholes
Bind off 6 sts at beg of next 2 rows. **43 (48: 53: 58) sts.**
Work even until back measures 10¹/₄ (11: 11³/₄: 12¹/₂)in from cast-on edge, ending with a p row.
Shape shoulders
Bind off 5 (6: 7: 8) sts at beg of next 4 rows.
Leave rem 23 (24: 25: 26) sts on a holder.

left front

With size 2 needles and C, cast on 44 (47: 50: 53) sts.
K 1 row.
Change to size 3 needles and M.
Beg with a k row, work in St st.
Work 6 (8: 10: 10) rows.
Dec row (right side) K8, skp, k to end.
Work 9 (9: 9: 11) rows.
Rep the last 10 (10: 10: 12) rows 3 times more and the dec row again. **39 (42: 45: 48) sts.**
Work even until front measures 6³/₄ (7: 8: 8¹/₄)in from cast-on edge, ending with a p row.
Shape armhole
Bind off 6 sts at beg of next row. **33 (36: 39: 42) sts.**
Next row P to end.
Buttonhole row K to last 4 sts, yo, k2tog, k2.
Next row P to end.
Next row K to end.
Shape neck
Next row (wrong side) Bind off 5 (6: 7: 8) sts, p to end. **28 (30: 32: 34) sts.**
K 1 row.
Next row Bind off 5 sts, p to end.
K 1 row.
Next row Bind off 3 sts, p to end. **20 (22: 24: 26) sts.**
Next row K to last 2 sts, k2tog.
Cont to dec 1 st at neck edge on every foll right-side row until 10 (12: 14: 16) sts rem.
Work even until front measures same as Back to shoulder, ending at armhole edge.
Shape shoulder
Bind off 5 (6: 7: 8) sts at beg of next row.
Work 1 row.
Bind off rem 5 (6: 7: 8) sts.

right front

With size 2 needles and C, cast on 44 (47: 50: 53) sts.
K 1 row.
Change to size 3 needles and M.
Beg with a k row, work in St st.
Work 6 (8: 10: 10) rows.
Dec row (right side) K to last 10 sts, k2tog, k8.
Work 9 (9: 9: 11) rows.
Rep the last 10 (10: 10: 12) rows 3 times more and the dec row again. **39 (42: 45: 48) sts.**
Work even until front measures 6³/₄ (7: 8: 8¹/₄)in from cast-on edge, ending with a k row.
Shape armhole
Bind off 6 sts at beg of next row. **33 (36: 39: 42) sts.**
Work even for 4 rows.
Shape neck
Next row (right side) Bind off 5 (6: 7: 8) sts, k to end. **28 (30: 32: 34) sts.**
P 1 row.
Next row Bind off 5 sts, k to end.
P 1 row.
Next row Bind off 3 sts, k to end. **20 (22: 24: 26) sts.**
P 1 row.
Next row Skp, k to end.
Cont to dec 1 st at neck edge on every foll right-side row until 10 (12: 14: 16) sts rem.
Work even until front measures same as Back to shoulder, ending at armhole edge.
Shape shoulder
Bind off 5 (6: 7: 8) sts at beg of next row.
Work 1 row.
Bind off rem 5 (6: 7: 8) sts.

sleeves

With size 2 needles and C, cast on 35 (38: 38: 41) sts.
K 1 row.
Change to size 3 needles and M.
Beg with a k row, work in St st and inc 1 st at each end of the 5th row and every foll 6th row until there are 45 (50: 50: 55) sts.
Work even until sleeve measures 4³/₄ (5: 5¹/₂: 6¹/₄)in from cast-on edge, ending with a p row.
Mark each end of last row with a colored thread.
Work ³/₄in more, ending with a p row.
Bind off.

button strip

With size 2 needles and M, cast on 15 (17: 19: 21) sts.
K 1 row.
Bind off.

right front edging	With right side facing, size 2 needles, and C, pick up and k 53 (55: 61: 63) sts evenly along right front edge. K 1 row. Bind off.
left front edging	With right side facing, size 2 needles, and C, pick up and k 53 (55: 61: 63) sts evenly along left front edge. K 1 row. Bind off.
neckband	Sew shoulder seams. With right side facing, size 2 needles, and C, pick up and k 1 st across row ends of right front band, 39 (42: 43: 46) sts up right front neck, k across 23 (24: 25: 26) sts from back neck holder, pick up and k 39 (42: 43: 46) sts down left front neck then pick up and k 1 st across row ends of front band. **103 (110: 113: 120) sts.** K 1 row. Bind off.
to finish	Sew sleeves to armholes, stitching row ends above markers to sts bound off at underarm. Sew side and sleeve seams. Cut ribbon in half and sew one piece to right front and one on left front. Sew one end of button strip to right front armhole seam 4 rows above armhole shaping, then sew button to other end.

sizes and measurements
To fit ages 0–3 (3–6: 6–9: 9–12) months
finished measurements
Around hips 16 (18: 20: 22)in
Length $11^{1}/_{2}$ (13: 15: 17)in

materials
2 (2: 2: 3) x $1^{3}/_{4}$ oz/50g balls Debbie Bliss Baby Cashmerino in chocolate (M) and small amount in lilac (C)
Pair each of sizes 2 and 3 knitting needles
Waist length of elastic, $^{1}/_{2}$in wide

gauge
25 sts and 34 rows to 4in square over St st using size 3 needles.

abbreviations
See page 25.

See page 25.

44

pants to match

legs (make 2)

With size 2 needles and C, cast on 54 (60: 66: 72) sts.
Rib row *K1, p1; rep from * to end.
Change to M and work 9 rows more in rib.
Change to size 3 needles, and beg with a k row, work in St st until work measures $5^{1}/_{2}$ ($6^{1}/_{4}$: $6^{3}/_{4}$: $7^{1}/_{2}$)in from cast-on edge, ending with a p row.
Shape crotch
Inc 1 st at each end of the next row and 2 (2: 3: 3) foll alt rows.
P 1 row.
Cast on 3 sts at beg of next 2 rows. **66 (72: 80: 86) sts.**
Shape for legs
Work 2 rows.
Dec 1 st at inside edge of the next row and 2 (3: 4: 5) foll alt rows. **60 (64: 70: 74) sts.**
Dec 1 st at each end of 5 (6: 7: 8) foll 6th rows. **50 (52: 56: 58) sts.**
Work 6 (6: 8: 10) rows.
Change to size 2 needles and C, and K 2 rows.
Bind off.

to finish

Sew inner leg seams. Sew center front and back seam. Sew ends of elastic together to form a ring, and sew it to wrong side of rib at waist by encasing it with herringbone stitches.

45

first coat

sizes and measurements
To fit ages 0–3 (3–6: 6–9: 9–12) months
finished measurements
Chest 18 (19³/₄: 21³/₄: 23¹/₂)in
Length to shoulder 11 (11³/₄: 12¹/₂: 13¹/₂)in
Sleeve length 4³/₄ (5: 5¹/₂: 6¹/₄)in

materials
3 (3: 4: 4) x 1³/₄oz/50g balls Debbie Bliss Baby Cashmerino in stone (M) and a small amount
in ecru (C)
Pair each of sizes 2 and 3 knitting needles
4 small buttons

gauge
25 sts and 34 rows to 4in square over St st, and 32 sts and 34 rows to 4in square over rib both
using size 3 needles.

abbreviations
See page 25.

back

With size 2 needles and M, cast on 75 (83: 91: 99) sts.
K 3 rows.
Change to size 3 needles.
Beg with a k row, work in St st until back measures 6 (6$^1/_4$: 7: 7$^1/_2$)in from cast-on edge, ending with a p row.
Next row (right side) K1, *p1, k1; rep from * to end.
Next row P1, *k1, p1; rep from * to end.
Rep the last 2 rows until back measures 7 (7$^1/_2$: 8$^3/_4$: 9)in from cast-on edge, ending with a wrong-side row.
Shape armholes
Bind off 8 sts at beg of next 2 rows. **59 (67: 75: 83) sts.**
Dec 1 st at each end of the next row and 3 (4: 5: 6) foll alt rows. **51 (57: 63: 69) sts.**
Work even until back measures 11 (11$^3/_4$: 12$^1/_2$: 13$^1/_2$)in from cast-on edge, ending with a wrong-side row.
Shape shoulders
Bind off 9 (11: 14: 16) sts at beg of next 2 rows.
Leave rem 33 (35: 35: 37) sts on a holder.

left front

With size 2 needles and M, cast on 39 (43: 47: 51) sts.
K 3 rows.
Change to size 3 needles.
Next row (right side) K to end.
Next row K3, p to end.
These 2 rows form the St st with garter st edging.
Work even until front measures 6 (6$^1/_4$: 7: 7$^1/_2$)in from cast-on edge, ending with a wrong-side row.
Next row (right side) *P1, k1; rep from * to last 5 sts, p1, k4.
Next row K3, *p1, k1; rep from * to end.
Rep the last 2 rows until front measures 7 (7$^1/_2$: 8$^3/_4$: 9)in from cast-on edge, ending with a wrong-side row.
Shape armhole
Bind off 9 sts at beg of next row. **30 (34: 38: 42) sts.**
Work 1 row.
Dec 1 st at beg of the next row and 3 (4: 5: 6) foll alt rows. **26 (29: 32: 35) sts.**
Work even until front measures 9$^1/_2$ (10$^1/_4$: 10$^3/_4$: 11$^1/_2$)in from cast-on edge, ending with a wrong-side row.
Shape neck
Next row Rib to last 10 sts, leave these sts on a holder.
Dec 1 st at neck edge on every row until 9 (11: 14: 16) sts rem.
Work even until front measures same as Back to shoulder, ending at armhole edge.
Shape shoulder
Bind off.
Mark positions for 4 buttons, the first on the 3rd row of rib patt and the fourth $^3/_8$in below neck shaping, with the rem 2 buttons spaced evenly between.

right front

With size 2 needles and M, cast on 39 (43: 47: 51) sts.

K 3 rows.

Change to size 3 needles.

Next row (right side) K to end.

Next row P to last 3 sts, k3.

These 2 rows form the St st with garter st edging.

Work even until front measures 6 (6^1/$_4$: 7: 7^1/$_2$)in from cast-on edge, ending with a wrong-side row.

Next row (right side) K4, p1, *k1, p1; rep from * to end.

Next row K1, *p1, k1; rep from * to last 4 sts, p1, k3.

Buttonhole row K2, yo, k2tog, p1, rib to end.

Work rem buttonholes as set by this row to match button markers.

Rep the last 2 rows until front measures 7 (7^1/$_2$: 8^3/$_4$: 9)in from cast-on edge, ending with a right-side row.

Shape armhole

Bind off 9 sts at beg of next row. **30 (34: 38: 42) sts.**

Dec 1 st at beg of the next row and 3 (4: 5: 6) foll alt rows. **26 (29: 32: 35) sts.**

Work even until front measures 9^1/$_2$ (10^1/$_4$: 10^3/$_4$: 11^1/$_2$)in from cast-on edge, ending with a wrong-side row.

Shape neck

Next row Rib 10 sts, leave these sts on a holder, rib to end.

Dec 1 st at neck edge on every row until 9 (11: 14: 16) sts rem.

Work even until front measures same as Back to shoulder, ending at armhole edge.

Shape shoulder

Bind off.

sleeves

With size 2 needles and M, cast on 40 (43: 45: 46) sts.
K 3 rows.
Change to size 3 needles.
Beg with a k row, work in St st and inc 1 st at each end of the 5th row and every foll 6th row until there are 50 (55: 57: 60) sts.
Work even until sleeve measures $4^3/_4$ (5: $5^1/_2$: $6^1/_4$)in from cast-on edge, ending with a p row.
Mark each end of last row with a colored thread.
Work $^3/_4$in more, ending with a p row.

Shape top of sleeve
Dec 1 st at each end of the next row and 3 (4: 5: 6) foll alt rows. **42 (45: 45: 46) sts.**
Bind off.

collar

Sew shoulder seams.
With right side facing, size 3 needles, and M, slip 10 sts from right front holder onto a needle, pick up and k 16 (16: 18: 18) sts up right front neck, k 33 (35: 35: 37) sts from back, 16 (16: 18: 18) sts down left side of front neck, k 10 sts from left front holder. **85 (87: 91: 93) sts.**
Next row (wrong side) K1, *p1, k1; rep from * to end.
This row sets the rib.
Next 2 rows Rib to last 26 sts, turn.
Next 2 rows Rib to last 20 sts, turn.
Next 2 rows Rib to last 14 sts, turn.
Next 2 rows Rib to last 8 sts, turn.
Next row Rib to end.
Bind off 4 sts at beg of next 2 rows.
Work 14 (16: 16: 18) rows more.
Break off yarn.
With right side facing, size 2 needles, and M, pick up and k 12 (14: 14: 16) sts along row ends of collar, k across sts of collar, then pick up and k 12 (14: 14: 16) sts along row ends of collar.
Next row K12 (14: 14: 16), M1, k to last 12 (14: 14: 16) sts, M1, k to end.
Change to C.
Next row K to end.
Next row K12 (14: 14: 16), M1, k to last 12 (14: 14: 16) sts, M1, k to end.
Bind off.

to finish

Sew sleeves to armholes, stitching row ends above markers to sts bound off at underarm. Sew side and sleeve seams. Sew on buttons. Sew row ends of collar edging in place.

home sweet home

size
Height 12in
Width 16^1/$_2$in

materials
1 x 1^3/$_4$oz/50g ball Debbie Bliss Rialto DK each in ecru (M), duck egg blue (A), pale pink (B), gray (C), and brown (D)
Pair of size 6 knitting needles
Plain birch picture frame, 11^3/$_4$in by 15^3/$_4$in

gauge
22 sts and 30 rows to 4in square over St st using size 6 needles.

abbreviations
See page 25.

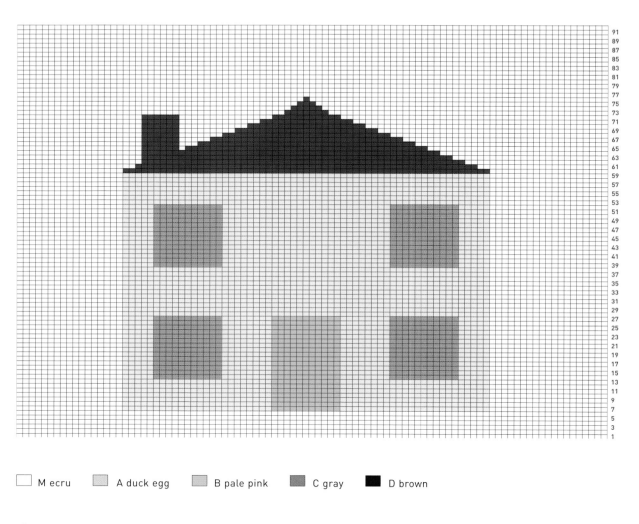

91
89
87
85
83
81
79
77
75
73
71
69
67
65
63
61
59
57
55
53
51
49
47
45
43
41
39
37
35
33
31
29
27
25
23
21
19
17
15
13
11
9
7
5
3
1

☐ M ecru   A duck egg   B pale pink   C gray   ■ D brown

chart note

The chart is worked in St st. When working from the chart, read k rows from right to left, and p rows from left to right. When working motif, use the intarsia method (see pages 28–30), knitting with a separate small ball of yarn for each area of color and twisting yarns on wrong side when changing color to avoid holes.

to make

With size 6 needles and M, cast on 95 sts.
Beg with a k row, work in St st from chart using the intarsia method, until all 92 rows have
been worked.
Bind off.

to finish

Press according to the yarn label. Remove glass from the frame, and cut a piece of cardboard
the same size as the backing board. Then using double-sided tape, secure the picture to the
cardboard, insert, and reassemble frame.

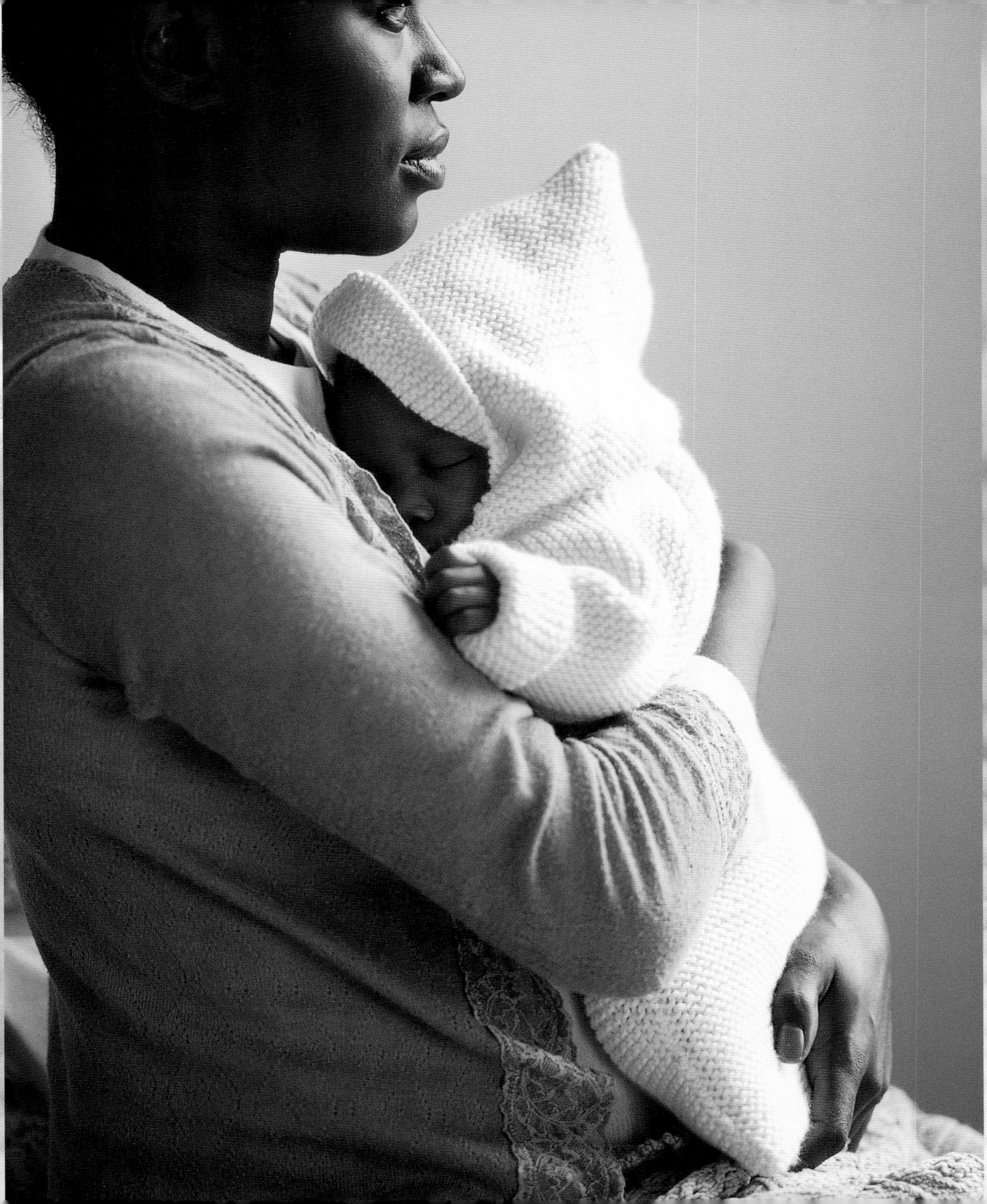

sizes and measurements
To fit ages 0–3 (3–6) months
finished measurements
Length to shoulder 21³/₄ (23¹/₂)in

materials
8 (9) x 1³/₄oz/50g balls Debbie Bliss Cashmerino Aran in ecru
Pair of size 7 knitting needles
Size 7 circular knitting needle
16in zipper

gauge
20 rows and 42 rows to 4in square over garter st using size 7 needles.

abbreviations
kfb = knit into front and back of next st.
See page 25.

hooded carrying bag

back, front, and sleeves
(worked in one piece)

With size 7 needles, cast on 54 (62) sts.
1st row Knit.
This row forms garter st and is repeated.
Work even until back measures 18 (19)in from cast-on edge, ending with a wrong-side row.
Change to size 7 circular needle.
Shape sleeves
Cast on 30 (36) sts at beg of next 2 rows. **114 (134) sts.**
Work even in garter st until back measures 21³/₄ (23¹/₂)in from cast-on edge, ending with a wrong-side row.
Place a marker at each end of last row for shoulder line.
Divide for fronts
Next row (right side) With size 7 needles, k43 (53), turn and cont on these sts only for right front, leaving rem sts on the circular needle.
Shape neck
Next row (wrong side) Kfb, k to end. **44 (54) sts.**
K 1 row.
Rep the last 2 rows once more. **45 (55) sts.**
Next row Cast on 2 sts, k to end. **47 (57) sts.**
K 1 row.
Next row Cast on 3 sts, k to end. **50 (60) sts.**

K 1 row.

Rep the last 2 rows once more. **53 (63) sts.**

Next row Cast on 7 sts, k to end. **60 (70) sts.**

Mark front edge of last row with a colored thread.

Work even in garter st until work measures 4 (4³/₄)in from shoulder line marker, ending with a wrong-side row.

Shape sleeve

Next row (right side) Bind off 30 (36) sts, k to end. **30 (34) sts.**

Cont in garter st until work measures 16in from front edge marker, ending with a right-side row.

Next row Bind off 3 sts, slip rem 27 (31) sts onto a holder.

Return to sts on circular needle and with right side facing, slip 28 sts at center back neck onto a holder, rejoin yarn to rem 43 (53) sts for left front, k to end.

K 1 row.

Next row (right side) Kfb, k to end. **44 (54) sts.**

K 1 row.

Rep the last 2 rows once more. **45 (55) sts.**

Next row Cast on 2 sts, k to end. **47 (57) sts.**

K 1 row.

Next row Cast on 3 sts, k to end. **50 (60) sts.**

K 1 row.

Rep the last 2 rows once more. **53 (63) sts.**

K 1 row.

Next row Cast on 4 sts, k to end. **57 (67) sts.**

Mark front edge of last row with a colored thread.

Work even in garter st until work measures 4 (4³/₄)in from shoulder line marker, ending with a right-side row.

Shape sleeve

Next row (wrong side) Bind off 30 (36) sts, k to end. **27 (31) sts.**

Cont in garter st until work measures 16in from front edge marker, ending with a right-side row.

Next row (wrong side) K 27 (31) sts of left front, then k across 27 (31) sts on right front holder. **54 (62) sts.**

Work even until front measures 21³/₄ (23¹/₂)in from shoulder line, ending with a right-side row.

Bind off.

hood

With right side facing and size 7 needles, pick up and k 22 sts up right front neck to shoulder, then work k2, [M1, k2] 13 times across 28 sts on back neck holder, then pick up and k 20 sts down left front neck. **83 sts.**

Work in garter st until hood measures 8in from pick-up row.

Bind off.

to finish

Fold bound-off edge of hood in half and sew together to form top seam. Fold along shoulder line and sew front to back along sleeve seams and around side and lower edges. Handstitch zipper in place, sewing left front edge close to the zipper teeth and right front edge approximately ³/₈in from the edge, to form a fly front. Sew bound-off sts of lower end of fly front in place.

lacy shawl

size
37in by 43in, excluding edging

materials
16 x 1³/₄oz/50g balls Debbie Bliss Baby Cashmerino in pale blue
Pair of size 3 knitting needles
Size 3 circular knitting needle

gauge
24 sts and 40 rows to 4in square over center lace patt using size 3 needles.

abbreviations
sk2p = sl 1, k2tog, pass slipped st over.
See page 25.

center piece

With size 3 circular needle, cast on 239 sts.
1st row (right side) K2, *k1 tbl, k2, yo, skp, k4, yo, skp, k3, k2tog, yo, k2; rep from * to last 3 sts, k1 tbl, k2.
2nd and every foll wrong-side row P.
3rd row K2, *k1, k2tog, yo, k1 tbl, yo, skp; rep from * to last 3 sts, k3.
5th row K1, yo, *sk2p, yo, k3, yo; rep from * to last 4 sts, sk2p, yo, k1.
7th row K2, *yo, skp, k3, k2tog, yo, k5, yo, skp, k4; rep from * to last 3 sts, yo, skp, k1.
9th row K2tog, yo, *k1 tbl, yo, skp, k3, k1 tbl, k2, yo, skp, k1, k1 tbl, k3, k2tog, yo; rep from * to last 3 sts, k1 tbl, yo, skp.
11th row K2, *k2, yo, skp, k3, k2tog, yo, k1 tbl, yo, skp, k3, k2tog, yo, k1; rep from * to last 3 sts, k3.
13th row K2, *k3, yo, skp, k1, k2tog, yo, k3, yo, skp, k1, k2tog, yo, k2; rep from * to last 3 sts, k3.
15th row K2, *[yo, skp, k2] twice, yo, sk2p, yo, k2, k2tog, yo, k3; rep from * to last 3 sts, yo, skp, k1.
17th row K2tog, yo, *k1 tbl, [yo, skp, k2] twice, yo, skp, k1, k2tog, yo, k2, k2tog, yo; rep from * to last 3 sts, k1 tbl, yo, skp.
19th row K2, *[k2, yo, skp] twice, k1, k1 tbl, k1, k2tog, yo, k2, k2tog, yo, k1; rep from * to last 3 sts, k3.
21st row K1, yo, *sk2p, yo, k5, yo, skp, k1, k2tog, yo, k5, yo; rep from * to last 4 sts, sk2p, yo, k1.
23rd row K2, *yo, skp, k6, yo, sk2p, yo, k7; rep from * to last 3 sts, yo, skp, k1.
24th row Rep 2nd row.
These 24 rows form the center patt and are repeated.
Cont in patt ending with the 23rd row of the 17th patt repeat (407 rows worked).
Bind off.

edging

With size 3 needles, cast on 10 sts.
K 1 row, then work in patt as follows:
1st row (wrong side) Sl 1, [k1, yo, k2tog] twice, k1, yo twice, k1, yo twice, k1.
2nd row [K2, p1] twice (each double yo is treated as 2 sts, the first is worked as k1, the second as p1), k2, [yo, k2tog, k1] twice.
3rd row Sl 1, [k1, yo, k2tog] twice, k7.
4th row Bind off 4, k3, [yo, k2tog, k1] twice.
Rep these 4 rows until border is long enough to fit all around edge of center piece, gathering slightly at the corners, ending with a 3rd row.
Bind off.

to finish

Block center piece by placing a towel over a board and pinning knitting out to the correct dimensions. Spray lightly with water and leave to dry. Cover border in sections with a damp cloth and press lightly with a medium iron. Sew together the cast-on and bound-off ends of the edging, then sew in place around the edge of the center piece.

size
Approximate height to shoulder 4in
Approximate length from nose to tail 5½in

materials
1 x 1¾oz/50g ball Debbie Bliss Cashmerino Astrakhan in ecru (A)
Scrap of double-knitting-weight yarn in black (B)
Pair of size 5 knitting needles
Washable toy filling (suitable for babies)

gauge
20 sts and 30 rows to 4in over St st using size 5 needles and yarn A.

abbreviations
kfb = k into front and back of next st.
pfb = p into front and back of next st.
sk2p = sl 1, k2tog, pass slipped st over.
See page 25.

toy lamb

main body
(worked from tail to nose)

**With size 5 needles and A, cast on 2 sts.
Beg with a k row, work in St st.
Work 2 rows.
Next row Kfb, kfb. **4 sts.****
P 1 row.
Next row (right side) Cast on 8 sts in A and 11 sts in B, k to end in correct yarns.
Next row Cast on 11 sts in B and 8 sts in A, p to end in correct yarns. **42 sts.**
Place a marker (X) on 14th st from each end of last row.
Work 4 rows in St st.
Bind off 7 sts at beg of next 2 rows. **28 sts.**
Next row Bind off 2 sts, k to last 2 sts, k2tog.
Next row Bind off 2 sts, p to last 2 rows, p2tog. **22 sts.**
Next row K2tog, k to last 2 sts, k2tog. **20 sts.**
Work 7 rows.
Cast on 3 sts in B at beg of next 2 rows and 8 sts in B at beg of foll 2 rows. **42 sts.**
Work 4 rows.
Bind off 14 sts at beg of next 2 rows. **14 sts.**
Work 2 rows.
Place a marker (Y) at each end of last row.

Shape head

Next row K4, [kfb, k1] twice, kfb, k5. **17 sts.**

Next row P5, [pfb, p1] 3 times, pfb, p5. **21 sts.**

K 1 row.

Next row P2tog, p to last 2 sts, p2tog.

Rep the last 2 rows once more. **17 sts.**

Next row K7 B, k3 A, k7 B.

Next row P8 B, p1 A, p8 B.

Work 2 rows.

Next row K2, skp, k1, skp, k3, k2tog, k1, k2tog, k2. **13 sts.**

P 1 row.

Next row K3, skp, k3, k2tog, k3. **11 sts.**

P 1 row.

Next row K1, [skp] twice, k1, [k2tog] twice, k1. **7 sts.**

Next row P1, p2tog, p1, p2tog tbl, p1. **5 sts.**

Next row K1, sk2p, k1. **3 sts.**

Break off yarn, thread through rem sts, pull to gather, and secure.

gusset
(worked from back to front)

With size 5 needles, cast on 11 B, 6 A, 11 B. **28 sts.**

Keeping yarns correct throughout and beg with a k, row work 4 rows in St st.

Next row Bind off 7 sts, with 1 st on needle after bind-off, k next 5 sts, k2tog, k to end.

Next row Bind off 7 sts, p to end. **13 sts.**

Next row Bind off 2 sts, k to last 2 sts, k2tog.

Next row Bind off 2 sts, p to last 2 sts, p2tog tbl. **7 sts.**

Next row K2tog, k to last 2 sts, k2tog. **5 sts.**

Cont in St st, work 7 rows.

Cast on 3 sts in B at beg of next 2 rows and 8 sts in B at beg of foll 2 rows. **27 sts.**

Work 4 rows.

Bind off 12 sts at beg of next 2 rows. **3 sts.**

Work 2 rows.

Next row Sk2p and fasten off.

ears (make 2)

With size 5 needles and B, cast on 2 sts.

K 2 rows.

Next row Kfb, k1. **3 sts.**

K 6 rows.

Bind off.

to finish

Sew head seam from nose to markers (Y). Sew back seam from tail to markers (X). Sew gusset to main body with point of gusset at markers (Y), center of cast-on edge of gusset at markers (X), and matching legs, but leaving seam open between legs on one side. Insert toy filling in legs first, then head, and finally body. Sew opening closes. Sew ears in place and embroider eyes with yarn A.

Romper panties   Baby shorts   Heart mobile
Bathrobe   Vest   Pinafore dress   Baby
beanbag   Felted slippers

at home

sizes and measurements
To fit ages 3–6 (6–9) months
finished measurements
Around hips 20 (22)in
Length 8¾ (9½)in

materials
2 (2) x 1¾oz/50g balls Debbie Bliss Baby Cashmerino in gray
Pair each of sizes 2 and 3 knitting needles
Waist length of elastic, ¾in wide

gauge
25 sts and 34 rows to 4in square over St st using size 3 needles.

abbreviations
See page 25.

romperpanties

back

With size 2 needles, cast on 66 (76) sts.
Rib row *K1, p1; rep from * to end.
Work 9 rows more in rib.
Change to size 3 needles.
Back shaping
Next 2 rows K to last 30 sts, turn, sl 1, p to last 30 sts, turn.
Next 2 rows Sl 1, k to last 24 sts, turn, sl 1, p to last 24 sts, turn.
Next 2 rows Sl 1, k to last 18 sts, turn, sl 1, p to last 18 sts, turn.
Next 2 rows Sl 1, k to last 12 sts, turn, sl 1, p to last 12 sts, turn.
Next 2 rows Sl 1, k to last 6 sts, turn, sl 1, p to last 6 sts, turn.
Next row Sl 1, k to end.
Inc row P3, M1, [p6, M1] 4 times, p12 (22), [M1, p6] 4 times, M1, p3. **76 (86) sts.**
Beg with a k row, cont in St st.
Work 42 (52) rows.
Dec 1 st at each end of the next row and 9 (7) foll alt rows. **56 (70) sts.**
P 1 row.
Dec 1 st at each end of the next 16 (20) rows. **24 (30) sts.**
Work 20 (22) rows without shaping.
Break off yarn and leave these sts on a holder.

Side of right leg
With size 3 needles, cast on 2 sts.
P 1 row.
Next row K1, M1, k1.
Next row P2, M1, p1.
Next row K1, M1, k to end.
Next row P to last st, M1, p1.
Rep the last 2 rows 10 (11) times. **26 (28) sts.**
Break off yarn and leave these sts on a holder.
Side of left leg
With size 3 needles, cast on 2 sts.
P 1 row.
Next row K1, M1, k1.
Next row P1, M1, p2.
Next row K to last st, M1, k1.
Next row P1, M1, p to end.
Rep the last 2 rows 10 (11) times. **26 (28) sts.**
Next row K these 26 (28) sts, k24 (30) sts from first holder, then k 26 (28) sts from second holder.
76 (86) sts.
Work 18 (26) rows without shaping.
Dec row [P5, p2tog] 5 times, p6 (16), [p2tog, p5] 5 times. **66 (76) sts.**
Change to size 2 needles.
Rib row *K1, p1; rep from * to end.
Work 9 rows more in rib.
Bind off in rib.

leg edgings

With right side facing and size 3 needles, pick up and k 72 (78) sts evenly around leg opening.
Rib row *K1, p1; rep from * to end.
Work 1 row more in rib.
Change to size 2 needles.
Work 3 rows more in rib.
Bind-off row Bind off 3 sts, *slip st back onto left-hand needle, cast on 2 sts onto left-hand needle, bind off 6 sts; rep from *, ending last rep bind off 3 sts.

to finish

Sew side and edging seams. Sew ends of elastic together to form a ring, and sew it to wrong side of rib at waist by encasing it with herringbone stitches.

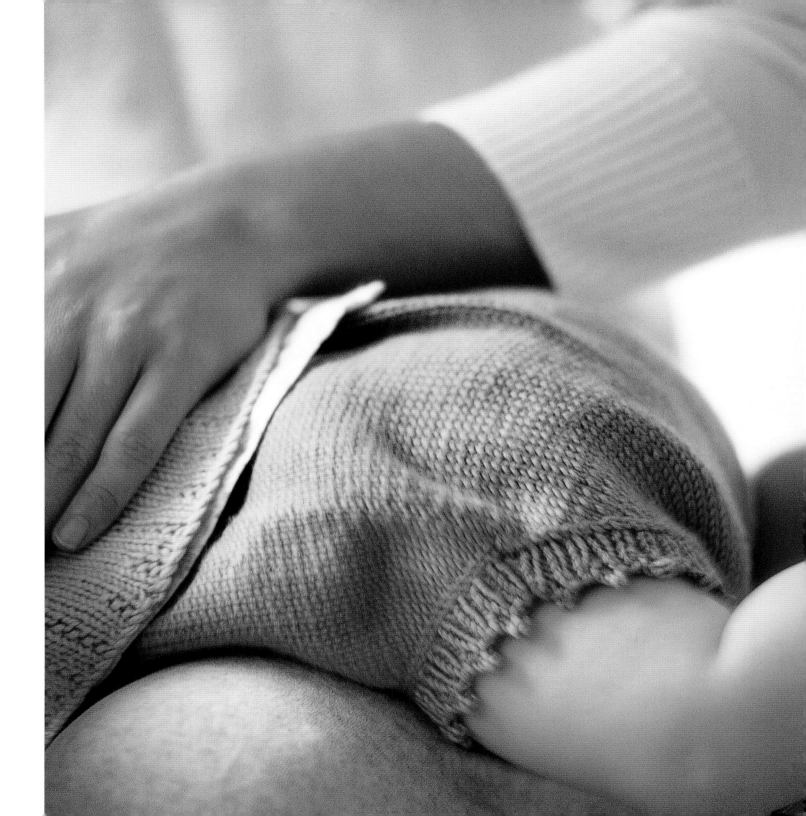

sizes and measurements
To fit ages 3–6 (6–9) months
finished measurements
Around hips 20 (22)in
Length 10³/₄ (11³/₄)in

materials
2 (3) x 1³/₄oz/50g balls Debbie Bliss Baby Cashmerino in gray
Pair each of sizes 2 and 3 knitting needles
Waist length of elastic, ³/₄in wide

gauge
25 sts and 34 rows to 4in square over St st using size 3 needles

abbreviations
See page 25.

baby shorts

right leg

With size 2 needles, cast on 66 (72) sts.
Rib row *K1, p1; rep from * to end.
Work 9 rows more in rib.
Change to size 3 needles.
Back shaping
Next 2 rows K6, turn, sl 1, p to end.
Next 2 rows K12, turn, sl 1, p to end.
Next 2 rows K18, turn, sl 1, p to end.
Next 2 rows K24, turn, sl 1, p to end.
Next 2 rows K30, turn, sl 1, p to end.
2nd size only
Next 2 rows K36, turn, sl 1, p to end.
Both sizes
Beg with a k row, cont in St st until work measures 6³/₄ (7¹/₂)in along short edge, ending with a p row.
**Shape crotch
Inc row (right side) K2, M1, k to last 2 sts, M1, k2.
P 1 row.
Rep the last 2 rows 3 times more. **74 (80) sts.**
Cast on 3 sts at beg of next 2 rows. **80 (86) sts.**

Shape for legs

Work 2 rows in St st.

Dec row (right side) K2, skp, k to last 4 sts, k2tog, k2.

Work 3 rows in St st.

Rep the last 4 rows 4 (5) times more. **70 (74) sts.**

Leg edging

Change to size 2 needles.

Dec row K1 (3), [k2tog, k4] 11 times, k2tog, k1 (3). **58 (62) sts.**

P 1 row.

Eyelet row (right side) K1, [yo, k2tog] to last st, k1.

Work 2 rows in St st.

Bind off.

left leg

With size 2 needles, cast on 66 (72) sts.

Rib row *K1, p1; rep from * to end.

Work 9 rows more in rib.

Change to size 3 needles.

Back shaping

Next 2 rows P6, turn, sl 1, k to end.

Next 2 rows P12, turn, sl 1, k to end.

Next 2 rows P18, turn, sl 1, k to end.

Next 2 rows P24, turn, sl 1, k to end.

Next 2 rows P30, turn, sl 1, k to end.

2nd size only

Next 2 rows P36, turn, sl 1, k to end.

Both sizes

Beg with a p row, cont in St st until work measures $6^3/_4$ ($7^1/_2$)in along short edge, ending with a p row.

Work as Right Leg from ** to end.

to finish

Sew inner leg seams. Sew center front and back seam. Sew ends of elastic together to form a ring, and sew it to wrong side of rib at waist by encasing it with herringbone stitches. Fold picot edge of legs to wrong side and slip stitch in place.

sizes
Approximately $3^1/_4$ ($3^1/_2$: 4)in for small (medium: large) hearts

materials
Small amount of Debbie Bliss Cotton DK each in ecru (A), duck egg blue (B), lime (C), and pale pink (D)
Pair of size 6 knitting needles
48in of narrow ribbon

gauge
20 sts and 28 rows to 4in square over St st using size 6 needles.

abbreviations
kfb = knit into front and back of next st.
ssk = [slip 1 knitwise] twice, insert tip of left hand needle into fronts of slipped sts and k2tog.
See page 25.

heart mobile

note
The instructions are given for the basic heart shapes and the charts are given for the designs we used for our shapes. You can draw out the shapes on graph paper and create your own designs. Carry yarns not in use across wrong side of work and weave in yarns if carried over more than 4 sts. When working large spots, twist yarns at color change to avoid holes forming.

basic hearts
(make 2 of each size)

With size 6 needles, cast on 2 sts.
1st row P2.
2nd row (right side) Kfb, kfb. 4 sts.
3rd row P.
4th row K1, M1, k to last st, M1, k1.
Rep the last 2 rows until there are 14 (16: 18) sts, ending with a right-side row.
Work 3 rows in St st.
Next row Rep 4th row. **16 (18: 20) sts.**
Work 3 (5: 5) rows in St st.
Small and medium hearts only
Next row Ssk, k4 (5), k2tog, turn and cont on these 6 (7) sts only.
P 1 row.
Next row Ssk, k4 (5).
P 1 row.

| □ A ecru | ▨ B duck egg | ▨ C lime | ▨ D pale pink |

Next row Ssk, k1 (2), k2tog.
P 1 row.
Bind off.
With right side facing, rejoin yarn to rem sts, ssk, k4 (5), k2tog.
P 1 row.
Next row K4 (5), k2tog.
P 1 row.
Next row Ssk, k1(2), k2tog.
P 1 row.
Bind off.
Large heart only
Next row Ssk, k to last 2 sts, k2tog. 18 sts.
P 1 row.
Next row Ssk, k5, k2tog, turn and cont on these 7 sts only.
**Work 3 rows in St st.
Next row Ssk, k3, k2tog.
P 1 row.
Bind off.**
With right side facing, rejoin yarn to rem sts, ssk, k5, k2tog.
Work as first side from ** to **.

to finish

Sew hearts together in pairs around their outer edges. Thread the ribbon through the small heart from top to bottom, leaving a loop at the top. Tie the two ends together under the heart to prevent it slipping down the ribbon. Thread the ribbon ends through the medium heart and tie at the base, then thread through the large heart and tie.

sizes and measurements
To fit ages 6 (12: 18: 24) months
finished measurements
Chest 23^1/$_4$ (24^3/$_4$: 26^1/$_2$: 28)in
Length to shoulder 16^1/$_2$ (19: 21^1/$_4$: 23^1/$_2$)in
Sleeve length (with cuff turned back) 6^1/$_4$ (7: 8^1/$_4$: 9^1/$_2$)in

materials
11 (12: 14: 15) x 1^3/$_4$oz/50g balls Debbie Bliss Cotton DK in pink (M), and one ball in chocolate (C)
Pair each of sizes 5 and 6 knitting needles
Size 6 circular knitting needle

gauge
20 sts and 32 rows to 4in square over seed st using size 6 needles.

abbreviations
See page 25.

bathrobe

back

With size 6 circular needle and M, cast on 157 (169: 185: 197) sts.
Seed st row K1, *p1, k1; rep from * to end.
This row forms the seed st and is repeated.
Work 31 (33: 35: 37) rows more in seed st.
Dec row (right side) Seed st 42 (44: 46: 48), k3tog, seed st to last 45 (47: 49: 51), k3tog, seed st to end.
Seed st 13 rows.
Dec row (right side) Seed st 41 (43: 45: 47), p3tog, seed st to last 44 (46: 48: 50), p3tog, seed st to end.
Seed st 13 rows.
Cont in seed st, dec 4 sts as set on next row and 1 (2: 3: 4) foll 14th rows, then work the dec row once more. **137 (145: 157: 165) sts.**
Work 11 rows.
Divide for back and fronts
Next row Seed st 36 (38: 41: 43) sts and leave these sts on a holder for right front, bind off next 6 (6: 8: 8) sts, with 1 st on needle after bind-off, seed st next 52 (56: 58: 62) sts and leave these sts on a holder for back, bind off next 6 (6: 8: 8) sts, with 1 st on needle after bind-off, seed st 35 (37: 40: 42). Working on the last set of 36 (38: 41: 43) sts for left front, work 4$\frac{1}{4}$ (4$\frac{3}{4}$: 5: 5$\frac{1}{2}$)in more in seed st, ending with a wrong-side row.
Shape shoulder
Bind off 16 (17: 18: 19) sts at beg of next row.
Work 1 row.
Leave rem 20 (21: 23: 24) sts on a spare needle.
Back
With wrong side facing, rejoin yarn to 53 (57: 59: 63) sts on back holder, patt to end.
Work even until back measures same as Left Front to shoulder, ending with a wrong-side row.
Shape shoulders
Bind off 16 (17: 18: 19) sts at beg of next 2 rows.
Bind off rem 21 (23: 23: 25) sts.
Right front
With wrong side facing, rejoin yarn to 36 (38: 41: 43) sts on right front holder, patt to end.
Work even until front measures same as Back to shoulder, ending with a right-side row.
Shape shoulder
Bind off 16 (17: 18: 19) sts at beg of next row. **20 (21: 23: 24) sts.**
Leave rem sts on a holder.

sleeves

With size 6 needles and C, cast on 29 (31: 33: 35) sts.
K 1 row.
Change to M.
Next row K1, *p1, k1; rep from * to end.
This row forms the seed st and is repeated.
Work 13 (13: 15: 15) rows more in seed st.
Change to size 5 needles.
Work 14 (14: 16: 16) rows.
Change to size 6 needles.
Cont in seed st and inc 1 st at each end of 3rd (5th: 5th: 7th) row and every foll 4th row until

there are 45 (49: 55: 59) sts, taking all inc sts into seed st.
Work even until sleeve measures 8 (8³/₄: 10¹/₄: 11¹/₂)in from cast-on edge, ending with a wrong-side row.
Mark each end of last row with a colored thread.
Work 6 (6: 8: 8) rows more.
Bind off.

hood

Sew shoulder seams.
Using size 6 needles and M, cont as follows:
Next row (right side) Seed st 20 (21: 23: 24) sts from right front, cast on 31 (35: 35: 39) sts, seed st 20 (21: 23: 24) sts from left front. **71 (77: 81: 87) sts.**
Work 60 (62: 64: 66) rows in seed st.
Shape top
Next row Seed st 34 (37: 39: 42), work 3 tog, seed st 34 (37: 39: 42).
Next row Seed st 33 (36: 38: 41), work 3 tog, seed st 33 (36: 38: 41).
Next row Seed st 32 (35: 37: 40), work 3 tog, seed st 32 (35: 37: 40).
Next row Seed st 31 (34: 36: 39), work 3 tog, seed st 31 (34: 36: 39).
Next row Seed st 30 (33: 35: 38), work 3 tog, seed st 30 (33: 35: 38).
Next row Seed st 29 (32: 34: 37), work 3 tog, seed st 29 (32: 34: 37).
Next row Seed st 28 (31: 33: 36), work 3 tog, seed st 28 (31: 33: 36).
Next row Seed st 27 (30: 32: 35), work 3 tog, seed st 27 (30: 32: 35).
Bind off.

pockets (make 2)

With size 6 needles and M, cast on 19 (21: 21: 23) sts.
Work 24 (26: 26: 28) rows in seed st.
Change to C.
K 1 row.
Bind off in C.

tie belt

With size 6 circular needle and M, cast on 191 (201: 211: 221) sts.
Work 3 rows in seed st.
Bind off in seed st.

to finish

Sew upper hood seam. Sew cast-on edge of hood to sts bound off at back neck. Sew sleeve seams to markers, reversing seam for turn-up. Sew sleeves to armholes, stitching row ends above markers to sts bound off at underarm. Sew on pockets.

sizes and measurements

To fit ages 0–3 (3–6: 6–9: 9–12:) months

finished measurements

Chest $17^3/_4$ ($19^3/_4$: 21: $22^3/_4$)in

Length to shoulder $8^1/_4$ ($9^1/_2$: $10^1/_4$: 11)in

materials

2 (2: 3: 3) x $1^3/_4$oz/50g balls Debbie Bliss Baby Cashmerino in flax

Pair each of sizes 2 and 3 knitting needles

Size 2 circular knitting needle

One small button

gauge

25 sts and 34 rows to 4in square over St st using size 3 needles.

abbreviations

See page 25.

vest

back

With size 3 needles, cast on 59 (65: 68: 74) sts.

1st row (right side) K2, *p1, k2; rep from * to end.

2nd row P.

Rep the last 2 rows twice more.

Now work in patt as follows:

1st row (right side) K2 (5: 2: 5), *p1, k8; rep from * to last 6 sts, p1, k2 (5: 2: 5).

2nd row P.

These 2 rows form the patt and are repeated.

Cont in patt until back measures 4¹/₄ (5: 5¹/₂: 6)in from cast-on edge, ending with a p row.

Shape armholes

Bind off 3 (4: 4: 5) sts at beg of next 2 rows. **53 (57: 60: 64) sts.**

Dec 1 st at each end of next row and 3 (3: 4: 4) foll alt rows. **45 (49: 50: 54) sts.****

Cont in patt until back measures 6 (6³/₄: 7¹/₂: 8³/₄)in from cast-on edge, ending with a wrong-side row.

Back neck opening

1st row (right side) Patt 22 (24: 25: 27) sts, turn and work on these sts only for first side of neck shaping, leaving rem sts on a spare needle.

2nd row Cast on 2 sts, then work k2, p to end. **24 (26: 27: 29) sts.**

Next row Patt to last 2 sts, k2.

Next row K2, p to end.

Rep the last 2 rows until back measures 7¹/₂ (8³/₄: 9¹/₂: 10¹/₄)in from cast-on edge, ending with a wrong-side row.

Shape neck

Next row K15 (16: 17: 18) sts, turn, leaving rem 9 (10: 10: 11) sts on a safety pin.

Next row P1, p2tog, p to end.

Next row Patt to last 3 sts, k2tog, k1.

Rep the last 2 rows once more. **11 (12: 13: 14) sts.**

Work 3 rows in patt.

Bind off for shoulder.

With right side facing, rejoin yarn to sts on spare needle, k2, patt to end.

Next row P to last 2 sts, k2.

Next row K2, patt to end.

Rep the last 2 rows until back measures 7¹/₂ (8³/₄: 9¹/₂: 10¹/₄)in from cast-on edge, ending with a right-side row.

Shape neck

Next row P12 (13: 14: 15) sts, p2tog tbl, p1, turn, leaving rem 8 (9: 9: 10) sts on a safety pin.

Next row K1, skp, patt to end.

Next row P to last 3 sts, p2tog tbl, p1.

Rep the last 2 rows once more. **11 (12: 13: 14) sts.**

Work 3 rows in patt.

Bind off for shoulder.

front

Work as given for Back to **.
Cont in patt until front measures 6 (7: 8: 8³/₄)in from cast-on edge, ending with a wrong-side row.

Shape neck
Next row K18 (20: 20: 22) sts, turn and work on these sts only for first side of front neck, leaving rem sts on a spare needle.
Next row Bind off 2 sts, p to end.
Patt 1 row.
Rep the last 2 rows once more. 14 (16: 16: 18) sts.
Next row P1, p2tog, p to end.
Patt 1 row.
Rep the last 2 rows 2 (3: 2: 3) times more. 11 (12: 13: 14) sts.
Work even until front measures same as Back to shoulder, ending with a p row.
Bind off for shoulder.
With right side facing, slip center 9 (9: 10: 10) sts onto a holder, rejoin yarn to rem sts on spare needle, patt to end.
Next row P.
Next row Bind off 2 sts, patt to end.
Rep the last 2 rows once more. 14 (16: 16: 18) sts.

Next row P to last 3 sts, p2tog tbl, p1.
Patt 1 row.
Rep the last 2 rows 2 (3: 2: 3) times more. 11 (12: 13: 14) sts.
Work even until front measures same as Back to shoulder, ending with a p row.
Bind off for shoulder.

neckband

Sew shoulder seams.
With right side facing and size 2 circular needle, slip 8 (9: 9: 10) sts from left back onto needle, pick
up and k 8 sts up left back neck, 21 sts down left side of front neck, k across 9 (9: 10: 10) sts from
front neck holder, pick up and k 21 sts up right side of front neck, 8 sts down right back neck, then
work p7 (8: 8: 9), k2 from back neck holder. 84 (86: 87: 89) sts.

1st and 3rd sizes only
1st row (wrong side) K2, p1, *k1, p2; rep from * to last 3 sts, k3.
2nd row (buttonhole row) K1, yo, p2tog, *k2, p1; rep from * to last 3 sts, k3.
3rd row K2, p1, *k1, p2; rep from * to last 3 sts, k3.
4th row K2, [p1, k2] 4 times, p1, [k2tog, p1, k2, p1] 4 times, k2tog, p1, k0 (-: 2: -), p0 (-: 1: -), k2tog,
[p1, k2, p1, k2tog] 4 times, [p1, k2] 5 times, k1.
Bind off knitwise.

2nd and 4th sizes only
1st row (wrong side) K2, p2, *k1, p2; rep from * to last 4 sts, k1, p1, k2.
2nd row (buttonhole row) K1, yo, k2tog, *p1, k2; rep from * to last 2 sts, k2.
3rd row K2, p2, *k1, p2; rep from * to last 4 sts, k1, p1, k2.
4th row K3, [p1, k2] 4 times, [k2tog, p1, k2, p1] 4 times, k2tog, p1, k- (0: -: 2), p- (0: -: 1), k2tog,
[p1, k2, p1, k2tog] 4 times, [p1, k2] 5 times, k2.
Bind off knitwise.

armbands

With right side facing and size 2 needles, pick up and k 65 (71: 77: 83) sts around armhole edge.
1st row (wrong side) P5, [k1, p2] to last 6 sts, k1, p5.
2nd row K5, *p1, k2; rep from * to last 6 sts, p1, k5.
3rd row Rep 1st row.

1st and 3rd sizes only
4th row K5, [p1, k2tog, p1, k2] 4 (-: 5: -) times, p1, [k2tog, p1] twice, [k2, p1, k2tog, p1] 4 (-: 5: -)
times, k5. 55 (-: 65: -) sts.

2nd and 4th sizes only
4th row K5, [p1, k2, p1, k2tog] – (5: -: 6) times, p1, [k2tog, p1, k2, p1] – (5: -: 6) times, k5.
– (61: -: 71) sts.

All sizes
Bind off knitwise.

to finish

Sew side and armband seams. Sew lower end of left back button band behind right back
buttonhole band. Sew on button.

pinafore dress

sizes and measurements
To fit ages 3–6 (6–9: 9–12) months
finished measurements
Chest 18^1/$_2$ (20^1/$_2$: 22^1/$_2$)in
Length to shoulder 14^1/$_4$ (16^1/$_2$: 19)in

materials
3 (4: 4) x 1^3/$_4$oz/50g balls Debbie Bliss Baby Cashmerino in gray
Pair each of sizes 2 and 3 knitting needles
2 buttons

gauge
25 sts and 40 rows to 4in over seed st using size 3 needles.

abbreviations
See page 25.

front

With size 2 needles, cast on 101 (109: 117) sts.

Beg with a k row, work in St st.

Work 2 rows.

Eyelet row K1, *yo, k2tog; rep from * to end.

Work 3 rows.

Change to size 3 needles.

Seed st row K1, *p1, k1; rep from * to end.

This row forms the seed st and is repeated.

Work even in seed st until front measures 8½ (10¼: 11¾)in from cast-on edge, ending with a wrong-side row.

Dec row (right side) K1 (2: 4), [skp, k1, k2tog] 20 (21: 22) times, k0 (2: 3). **61 (67: 73) sts.**

Change to 3mm needles.**

K 5 rows.

Bind off 8 (9: 10) sts at beg of next 2 garter st rows. **45 (49: 53) sts.**

Change to size 3 needles.

Next row K3, *p1, k1; rep from * to last 4 sts, p1, k3.

This row forms the seed st with garter st borders.

Patt 1 row.

Next row K2, skp, patt to last 4 sts, k2tog, k2.

Patt 3 rows.

Rep the last 4 rows 6 (7: 8) times more. **31 (33: 35) sts.**

Patt 1 row.

Change to size 2 needles.

K 5 rows.

Straps

Next row (right side) K6, turn.

Work on these 6 sts only for first strap until strap measures 10 (10¾: 11½)in.

Bind off.

With right side facing, rejoin yarn to rem sts, bind off 19 (21: 23) sts, k to end.

Work on rem 6 sts for second strap until strap measures 10 (10¾: 11½)in.

Bind off.

back

Work as given for Front to **.

K 3 rows.

Buttonhole row K15 (17: 19), yo, k2tog, k to last 17 (19: 21) sts, k2tog, yo, k15 (17: 19).

K 3 rows.

Bind off.

to finish

Sew side seams. Fold hem to wrong side and sew in place. Sew buttons to ends of straps to fit.

size
27^{1}/$_{2}$in by 27^{1}/$_{2}$in

materials
11 x 1^{3}/$_{4}$oz/50g balls Debbie Bliss Cotton DK in lime
Pair of size 6 knitting needles
Two pieces of cotton lining fabric, each 28^{1}/$_{2}$in square
Polystyrene beads
Two pieces of fabric for beanbag back, each 14^{3}/$_{4}$in by 28^{1}/$_{2}$in
26in zipper

gauge
20 sts and 32 rows to 4in square over seed st using size 6 needles.

abbreviations
See page 25.

baby beanbag

lining bag
With right sides of lining fabric pieces together and taking ^{1}/$_{2}$in seams, stitch around edges, leaving a 3^{1}/$_{4}$in opening in one side. Turn right side out and pour in the polystyrene beads; do not overfill—leave enough room for the beads to move around so that they will support the baby. (Use a cone of paper as a funnel when pouring in the beads and hold the open edges of the seam together when testing whether the bag is full enough.) Sew the opening in the seam closed.

beanbag front
With size 6 needles, cast on 141 sts.
Seed st row K1, *p1, k1; rep from * to end.
This row forms seed st and is repeated.
Work in seed st until work measures 27^{1}/$_{2}$in from cast-on edge.
Bind off in seed st.

beanbag back
With right sides together, pin and baste the two fabric back pieces together, taking a ^{1}/$_{2}$in seam allowance. Remove pins and sew the seam, leaving the center 26in unstitched for zipper. Press seam open. Lay zipper face down on the pressed seam and baste in place. From the right side, top-stitch the zipper in place. Remove all basting threads. Zigzag stitch around outer edge to reduce fraying of fabric.

to finish
With right sides together, lay knitted front on back and stitch around the outer edge, taking 1 seed st into the seam. Open zipper and turn beanbag right side out. Insert filled lining bag, close zipper.

felted slippers

size
To fit 0–3 months

materials
2 x 1^3/$_4$ oz/50 g balls Debbie Bliss Alpaca Silk Aran in stone
Pair of size 8 knitting needles

gauge
18 sts and 34 rows to 4in square over garter st using size 8 needles.

abbreviations
kfb = knit into front and back of next st.
See page 25.

note
The slippers will look very large and very floppy when knitted, but after washing they will shrink
and the fabric will become very thick and resilient.

slipper (make 2)

With size 8 needles, cast on 24 sts.
K 1 row.
Next row Cast on 2 sts, k to end.
Rep this row once more. **28 sts.**
Next row Kfb, k to last 2 sts, kfb, k1.
K 1 row.
Rep the last 2 rows, 3 times more. **36 sts.**
Place a marker at each end of last row.
K 4 rows.
Shape instep
Next row (right side) K24, turn.
Next row K12, turn.
K 18 rows on these 12 sts only.
Break yarn.
With right side facing, rejoin yarn at base of instep and pick up and k 9 sts along side edge of instep, k across 12 sts of instep, pick up and k 9 sts along other side of instep, then k rem 12 sts. **54 sts.**
K 9 rows.
Break off yarn.
Shape sole
Next row With right side facing, slip first 21 sts onto right-hand needle, rejoin yarn and k12, turn.
Next row K11, k2tog, turn.
Rep the last row 41 times more. **12 sts.**
Next row *K2tog; rep from * to end. **6 sts.**
Next row [K3tog] twice. **2 sts.**
Break off yarn, thread through rem sts, pull to gather, and secure, then sew back seam to markers. Weave in all yarn ends.

to felt

Wash the slippers in the washing machine at 175–200°F together with something heavy—for example, an old pair of jeans or anything that will withstand a very hot wash without losing any dye. When removed from the machine, the slippers will have shrunk considerably. Pull them into shape before leaving to dry.

Reversible hat   Classic cardigan   Stroller
blanket   Shawl collar sweater   Cable socks
Duffle coat   Changing mat bag

on the go

reversible hat

sizes
To fit ages 3–6 (9–12) months

materials
1 (2) x 1¾ oz/50 g balls Debbie Bliss Baby Cashmerino in each of lime (A) and gray (B)
Pair of size 3 knitting needles

gauge
26 sts and 34 rows to 4in square over 3 x 1 broken rib and 28 sts and 34 rows to 4in square over
1 x 1 broken rib, both using size 3 needles.

abbreviations
See page 25.

inner/outer hat

With size 3 needles and A, cast on 98 (106) sts.

1st row (right side) *K3, p1; rep from * to last 2 sts, k2.

2nd row Purl.

Rep these 2 rows until hat measures 5¹/₂ (6)in, ending with a p row.

1st dec row (right side) *K3, p1, k1, k2tog, p1; rep from * to last 2 sts, k2. **86 (93) sts.**

Patt 3 rows as set.

2nd dec row *K1, k2tog, p1, k2, p1; rep from * to last 2 sts, k2. **74 (80) sts.**

Patt 3 rows as set.

3rd dec row *K2, p1, k2tog, p1; rep from * to last 2 sts, k2. **62 (67) sts.**

Patt 3 rows as set.

4th dec row *K2tog, p1, k1, p1; rep from * to last 2 sts, k2. **50 (54) sts.**

P 1 row.

5th dec row K1, *k2tog, p1, k1; rep from * to last st, k1. **38 (41) sts.**

P 1 row.

6th dec row *K2tog, p1; rep from * to last 2 sts, k2. **26 (28) sts.**

P 1 row.

7th dec row K1, *k2tog; rep from * to last st, k1. **14 (15) sts.**

P 1 row.

8th dec row K1, *k2tog; rep from * to last st, k1(0). **8 sts.**

Break off yarn, thread through rem sts, pull to gather, secure, and sew seam.

outer/inner hat

With size 3 needles and B, cast on 104 (112) sts.

1st row (right side) *K1, p1; rep from * to end.

2nd row Purl.

Rep these 2 rows until hat measures 5¹/₂ (6)in, ending with a p row.

1st dec row (right side) *[K1, p1] twice, k1, k2tog, p1; rep from * to end. **91 (98) sts.**

Patt 3 rows.

2nd dec row *K1, k2tog, p1, k2, p1; rep from * to end. **78 (84) sts.**

Patt 3 rows.

3rd dec row *K2, p1, k2tog, p1; rep from * to end. **65 (70) sts.**

Patt 3 rows.

4th dec row *K2tog, p1, k1, p1; rep from * to end. **52 (56) sts.**

P 1 row.

5th dec row *K1, k2tog, p1; rep from * to end. **39 (42) sts.**

P 1 row.

6th dec row *K2tog, p1; rep from * to end. **26 (28) sts.**

P 1 row.

7th dec row K1, *k2tog; rep from * to last st, k1. **14 (15) sts.**

P 1 row.

8th dec row K0 (1), *k2tog; rep from * to end. **7 (8) sts.**

Break off yarn, thread through rem sts, pull to gather, secure, and sew seam.

to finish

Turn inner/outer hat wrong side out, place this inside the outer/inner hat, and slip stitch the hat pieces together all around the cast-on edges. Turn up the brim.

classic cardigan

sizes and measurements
To fit ages 0–3 (3–6: 6–9: 9–12) months
finished measurements
Chest 16$\frac{1}{2}$ (18: 19$\frac{3}{4}$: 21$\frac{1}{4}$)in
Length to shoulder 8 (8$\frac{3}{4}$: 9$\frac{3}{4}$: 11)in
Sleeve length 4$\frac{3}{4}$ (5$\frac{1}{2}$: 6$\frac{1}{4}$: 7)in

materials
3 (3: 3: 4) x 1$\frac{3}{4}$oz/50g balls Debbie Bliss Baby Cashmerino in flax
Pair each of sizes 2 and 3 knitting needles
5 small buttons

gauge
25 sts and 34 rows to 4in square over St st using size 3 needles.

abbreviations
See page 25.

back

With size 2 needles, cast on 54 (58: 62: 66) sts.
1st rib row (right side) K2, *p2, k2; rep from * to end.
2nd rib row P2, *k2, p2; rep from * to end.
Rep the last 2 rows twice more, inc 1 (2: 3: 4) sts evenly across last row. **55 (60: 65: 70) sts.**
Change to size 3 needles.
Beg with a k row, work in St st until back measures 4 (4$\frac{1}{4}$: 5: 6)in from cast-on edge, ending with a p row.
Shape underarm
Bind off 4 sts at beg of next 2 rows. **47 (52: 57: 62) sts.**
Leave these sts on a spare needle.

left front

With size 2 needles, cast on 27 (27: 31: 35) sts.
1st rib row (right side) K2, *p2, k2; rep from * to last 5 sts, p2, k3.
2nd rib row P3, *k2, p2; rep from * to end.
Rep the last 2 rows twice more, inc 1 (3: 2: 0) sts evenly across last row. **28 (30: 33: 35) sts.**
Change to size 3 needles.
Beg with a k row, work in St st until front measures 4 (4$\frac{1}{4}$: 5: 6)in from cast-on edge, ending with a p row.
Shape underarm
Bind off 4 sts at beg of next row. **24 (26: 29: 31) sts.**
Leave these sts on a spare needle.

right front

With size 2 needles, cast on 27 (27: 31: 35) sts.
1st rib row (right side) K3, *p2, k2; rep from * to end.

2nd rib row P2, *k2, p2; rep from * to last 5 sts, k2, p3.

Rep the last 2 rows twice more, inc 1 (3: 2: 0) sts evenly across last row. **28 (30: 33: 35) sts.**

Change to size 3 needles.

Beg with a k row, work in St st until front measures 4 (4¼: 5: 6)in from cast-on edge, ending with a k row.

Shape underarm

Bind off 4 sts at beg of next row. **24 (26: 29: 31) sts.**

P 1 row,

Leave these sts on a spare needle.

sleeves

With size 2 needles, cast on 34 (38: 38: 42) sts.

1st rib row K2, *p2, k2; rep from * to end.

2nd rib row P2, *k2, p2; rep from * to end.

Rep the last 2 rows twice more, inc 3 (0: 3: 2) sts evenly across last row. **37 (38: 41: 44) sts.**

Change to size 3 needles.

Beg with a k row, work in St st.

Work 4 rows.

Inc row K3, M1, k to last 3 sts, M1, k3.

Work 5 rows.

Rep the last 6 rows until there are 45 (50: 55: 60) sts.

Work even until sleeve measures 4³/₄ (5¹/₂: 6¹/₄: 7)in from cast-on edge, ending with a p row.
Shape underarm
Bind off 4 sts at beg of next 2 rows. **37 (42: 47: 52) sts.**
Leave these sts on a spare needle.

yoke

With right side facing and size 3 needles, k across 24 (26: 29: 31) sts from right front,
37 (42: 47: 52) sts from right sleeve, 47 (52: 57: 62) sts from back, 37 (42: 47: 52) sts from left sleeve,
24 (26: 29: 31) sts from left front. **169 (188: 209: 228) sts.**
Next row (wrong side) P to end.
Next row K21 (23: 26: 28), k2tog, k2, skp, k31 (36: 41: 46), k2tog, k2, skp, k41 (46: 51: 56), k2tog,
k2, skp, k31 (36: 41: 46), k2tog, k2, skp, k21 (23: 26: 28).
Work 3 rows.
Next row K20 (22: 25: 27), k2tog, k2, skp, k29 (34: 39: 44), k2tog, k2, skp, k39 (44: 49: 54), k2tog,
k2, skp, k29 (34: 39: 44), k2tog, k2, skp, k20 (22: 25: 27).
Next row P to end.
Next row K19 (21: 24: 26), k2tog, k2, skp, k27 (32: 37: 42), k2tog, k2, skp, k37 (42: 47: 52), k2tog,
k2, skp, k27 (32: 37: 42), k2tog, k2, skp, k19 (21: 24: 26).
Next row P to end.
Next row K18 (20: 23: 25), k2tog, k2, skp, k25 (30: 35: 40), k2tog, k2, skp, k35 (40: 45: 50), k2tog,
k2, skp, k25 (30: 35: 40), k2tog, k2, skp, k18 (20: 23: 25).
Next row P to end.
Cont in this way decreasing 8 sts on every right-side row until 65 (68: 73: 76) sts rem, ending with
a k row.
Next row P to end, decreasing 1 (0: 1: 0) st at center back. **64 (68: 72: 76) sts.**
Change to size 2 needles.
1st rib row (right side) K3, *p2, k2; rep from * to last 5 sts, p2, k3.
2nd rib row P3, *k2, p2; rep from * to last 5 sts, k2, p3.
Rep the last 2 rows twice more.
Bind off in rib.

button band

With right side facing and size 2 needles, pick up and k 58 (62: 70: 78) sts evenly along left front edge.
1st rib row P2, *k2, p2; rep from * to end.
2nd rib row K2, *p2, k2; rep from * to end.
Rep the last 2 rows once more and the first row again.
Bind off in rib.

buttonhole band

With right side facing and size 2 needles, pick up and k 58 (62: 70: 78) sts evenly along right front edge.
1st rib row (wrong side) P2, *k2, p2; rep from * to end.
2nd rib row K2, *p2, k2; rep from * to end.
Buttonhole row (wrong side) Rib 2, [rib 2tog, yo, rib 11 (12: 14: 16] 4 times, k2tog, yo, p2.
Work 2 rows more in rib.
Bind off in rib.

to finish

Sew side and sleeve seams. Sew underarm seams. Sew on buttons.

stroller blanket

size
Approximately 17³/₄in by 28in

materials
2 x 1³/₄oz/50g balls Debbie Bliss Cashmerino Aran each in pale blue (A) and lilac (C), and one ball each in mid blue (B), pale green (D), and mid green (E)
Pair of size 8 knitting needles or size 8 circular knitting needle

gauge
18 sts and 24 rows to 4in over St st using size 8 needles.

abbreviations
See page 25.

note
Use the intarsia method (see pages 28–30), knitting with a separate small ball of yarn for each area of color and twisting yarns on wrong side when changing color to avoid holes.

front

With size 8 needles and A, cast on 83 sts.
1st row K1, *p1, k1; rep from * to end.
Rep the last row 3 times more.
1st line
Next row (right side) With A [k1, p1] twice, k15 E, k15 D, k15 C, k15 B, k15 A, with A [p1, k1] twice.
Next row With A [k1, p1] twice, p15 A, p15 B, p15 C, p15 D, p15 E, with A [p1, k1] twice.
These 2 rows set the position of the 1st line of St st squares (with 4 seed sts in A at each side) and are repeated.
Work 18 rows more.

2nd line

Next row (right side) With A [k1, p1] twice, k15 B, k15 A, k15 E, k15 D, k15 C, with A [p1, k1] twice.
Next row With A [k1, p1] twice, p15 C, p15 D, p15 E, p15 A, p15 B, with A [p1, k1] twice.
These 2 rows set the position of the 2nd line of St st squares (with 4 seed sts in A at each side) and are repeated.
Work 18 rows more.

3rd line

Next row (right side) With A [k1, p1] twice, k15 C, k15 D, k15 B, k15 A, k15 E, with A [p1, k1] twice.
Next row With A [k1, p1] twice, p15 E, p15 A, p15 B, p15 D, p15 C, with A [p1, k1] twice.
These 2 rows set the position of the 3rd line of St st squares (with 4 seed sts in A at each side) and are repeated.
Work 18 rows more.

4th line

Next row (right side) With A [k1, p1] twice, k15 A, k15 E, k15 C, k15 D, k15 B, with A [p1, k1] twice.
Next row With A [k1, p1] twice, p15 B, p15 D, p15 C, p15 E, p15 A, with A [p1, k1] twice.
These 2 rows set the position of the 4th line of St st squares (with 4 seed sts in A at each side) and are repeated.
Work 18 rows more.

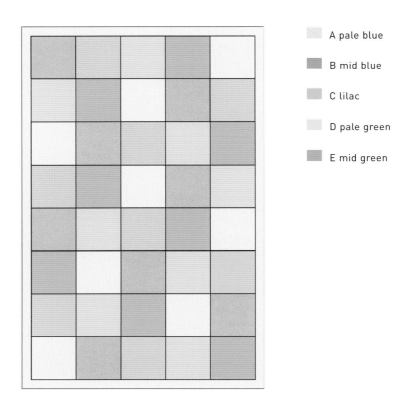

A pale blue

B mid blue

C lilac

D pale green

E mid green

5th line

Next row (right side) With A [k1, p1] twice, k15 D, k15 B, k15 A, k15 E, k15 C, with A [p1, k1] twice.

Next row With A [k1, p1] twice, p15 C, p15 E, p15 A, p15 B, p15 D, with A [p1, k1] twice.

These 2 rows set the position of the 5th line of St st squares (with 4 seed sts in A at each side) and are repeated.

Work 18 rows more.

6th line

Next row (right side) With A [k1, p1] twice, k15 E, k15 D, k15 C, k15 B, k15 A, with A [p1, k1] twice.

Next row With A [k1, p1] twice, p15 A, p15 B, p15 C, p15 D, p15 E, with A [p1, k1] twice.

These 2 rows set the position of the 6th line of St st squares (with 4 seed sts in A at each side) and are repeated.

Work 18 rows more.

7th line

Next row (right side) With A [k1, p1] twice, k15 C, k15 B, k15 A, k15 E, k15 D, with A [p1, k1] twice.

Next row With A [k1, p1] twice, p15 D, p15 E, p15 A, p15 B, p15 C, with A [p1, k1] twice.

These 2 rows set the position of the 7th line of St st squares (with 4 seed sts in A at each side) and are repeated.

Work 18 rows more.

8th line

Next row (right side) With A [k1, p1] twice, k15 A, k15 E, k15 D, k15 C, k15 B, with A [p1, k1] twice.

Next row With A [k1, p1] twice, p15 A, p15 B, p15 C, p15 D, p15 E, with A [p1, k1] twice.

These 2 rows set the position of the 8th line of St st squares (with 4 seed sts in A at each side) and are repeated.

Work 18 rows more.

Next row (right side) With A [k1, p1] twice, k75 A, with A [p1, k1] twice.

Next row With A, k1, *p1, k1; rep from * to end.

Rep the last row 3 times more.

Bind off in seed st.

back

With size 8 needles and A, cast on 83 sts.

1st row K1, *p1, k1; rep from * to end.

Rep the last row 3 times more.

Next row (right side) With A [k1, p1] twice, k75 E, with A [p1, k1] twice.

Next row With A [k1, p1] twice, p75 E, with A [p1, k1] twice.

These 2 rows form the St st with seed st edges in A and are repeated, working stripes as follows:

Keeping the seed st edges in A throughout, work 18 rows more in E, then work in 20 row stripes of C, A, D, B, C, D, E, ending with a wrong-side row.

Next row (right side) With A [k1, p1] twice, k75 A, with A [p1, k1] twice.

Next row With A, k1, *p1, k1; rep from * to end.

Rep the last row 3 times more.

Bind off in seed st.

to finish

Sew Back to Front around edges.

shawl collar sweater

sizes and measurements
To fit ages 3–6 (6–9: 9–12: 12–18: 18–24) months
finished measurements
Chest 19¾ (20¾: 23½: 24¾: 27½)in
Length to shoulder 9½ (10¼: 11½: 12½: 14¼)in
Sleeve length (with cuff turned back) 5½ (6¼: 7: 8: 8¾)in

materials
3 (4: 5: 5: 6) x 1¾oz/50g balls Debbie Bliss Cashmerino Aran in stone
Pair each sizes 7 and 8 knitting needles

gauge
24 sts and 24 rows to 4in square over rib when slightly stretched using size 8 needles.

abbreviations
See page 25.

back
With size 8 needles, cast on 62 (66: 74: 78: 86) sts.
1st row (right side) K2, *p2, k2; rep from * to end.
2nd row P2, *k2, p2; rep from * to end.
These 2 rows form the rib.
Cont in rib until back measures 5½ (6: 6¾: 7: 8¼)in from cast-on edge, ending with a wrong-side row.
Shape armholes
Bind off 3 sts at beg of next 2 rows. **56 (60: 68: 72: 80) sts.****
Cont in rib until back measures 9½ (10¼: 11½: 12½: 14¼)in from cast-on edge, ending with a wrong-side row.
Shape shoulders
Next row Bind off 17 (18: 21: 22: 25) sts, rib to last 17 (18: 21: 22: 25) sts and bind off these sts.
Leave rem 22 (24: 26: 28: 30) sts on a holder for collar.

front
Work as given for Back to **.
Shape neck
Next row Patt 21 (23: 27: 29: 33) sts, turn and work on these sts only for first side of neck shaping.
Work 1 row.
Dec 1 st at neck edge on next row and 3 (4: 5: 6: 7) foll 4th rows. **17 (18: 21: 22: 25) sts.**
Work even until front measures same as Back to shoulder, ending with a wrong-side row.
Bind off.
With right side facing, rejoin yarn to rem sts, bind off 14 sts, patt to end.
Complete to match first side of neck shaping.

sleeves
With size 8 needles, cast on 42 (46: 50: 54: 58) sts.
1st row (right side) K2, *p2, k2; rep from * to end.
2nd row P2, *k2, p2; rep from * to end.

These 2 rows form the rib.

Work 6 rows more in rib.

Change to size 7 needles and work 8 rows more in rib.

Change to size 8 needles.

Cont in rib, inc 1 st at each end of the 5th row and every foll 4th row until there are 54 (60: 66: 74: 78) sts.

Work even until sleeve measures 7$^1/_2$ (8$^1/_4$: 9: 10: 10$^3/_4$)in from cast-on edge, ending with a wrong-side row.

Place markers at each end of last row.

Work 4 rows more.

Bind off.

shawl collar

With right side facing and size 7 needles, rejoin yarn to 22 (24: 26: 28: 30) sts at back neck, cast on 4 (5: 4: 5: 4) sts, k2, p2, k0 (1: 0: 1: 0) across these sts, rib to end.

Next row (wrong side) Cast on 4 (5: 4: 5: 4) sts, p2, k2, p0 (1: 0: 1: 0) across these sts, rib to end.

Next row Cast on 4 sts, p2, k2, across these 4 sts, rib to end.

Next row Cast on 4 sts, k2, p2, across these 4 sts, rib to end.

Rep the last 2 rows 4 times more   **70 (74: 74: 78: 78) sts.**

Work even in rib for 10 rows.

Change to size 8 needles.

Work 2 rows more in rib.

Bind off loosely but evenly in rib.

to finish

Sew shoulder seams. Sew sleeves to armholes, stitching row ends above markers to sts bound off at underarm. Sew side and sleeve seams, reversing seam for cuff. Sew cast-on edge of collar to neck edge, overlap right side of collar over left, and sew row ends of collar to fronts.

126 cable socks

size
To fit ages 3–6 months

materials
1 x 1¾oz/50g ball Debbie Bliss Cashmerino DK in lilac
Pair of size 6 knitting needles
Cable needle

gauge
22 sts and 30 rows to 4in square over St st using size 6 needles.

abbreviations
C4B = slip next 2 sts onto cable needle and hold at back of work, k2, then k2 from cable needle.
pfb = purl into front and back of next st.
See page 25.

sock (make 2)

With size 6 needles, cast on 42 sts.
1st row K2, *p1, k4, p1, k2; rep from * to end.
2nd row P2, *k1, p4, k1, p2; rep from * to end.
3rd row K2, *p1, C4B, p1, k2; rep from * to end.
4th row Rep 2nd row.
These 4 rows form the cable patt and are repeated.
Rep 1st–4th rows once more, then the first 3 rows again.
Ridge row K4, *k2tog, k6; rep from * to last 6 sts, k2tog, k4. **37 sts.**
Inc row *P2, k1, p1, pfb, p1, k1; rep from * to last 2 sts, p2. **42 sts.**
Beg with a 1st row, rep the 4 cable patt rows 4 times more, then rep the first 3 patt rows again.

1st dec row P2, *k1, p2tog, p2tog, k1, p2; rep from * to end. **32 sts.**

2nd dec row K3, *k2tog, k6; rep from * to last 5 sts, k2tog, k3. **28 sts.**

Shape heel

Next row P8, turn.

Work 9 rows more in St st on these 8 sts only.

Dec row P2, p2tog, p1, turn.

Next row Sl 1, k3.

Dec row P3, p2tog, p1, turn.

Next row Sl 1, k4.

Dec row P4, p2tog.

Leave rem 5 sts on a holder.

With wrong side facing, slip center 12 sts onto a holder, rejoin yarn to rem 8 sts, p to end.

Work 8 rows more in St st on these 8 sts only.

Dec row K2, k2tog tbl, k1, turn.

Next row Sl 1, p3.

Dec row K3, k2tog tbl, k1, turn.

Next row Sl 1, p4.

Dec row K4, k2tog tbl, turn.

Next row Sl 1, p4.

Shape instep

Next row K5, pick up and k 8 sts evenly along inside edge of heel, k 12 sts from holder, pick up and k 8 sts evenly along inside edge of heel, then k 5 sts from holder. **38 sts.**

P 1 row.

Dec row K11, k2tog, k12, k2tog tbl, k11.

P 1 row.

Dec row K10, k2tog, k12, k2tog tbl, k10.

P 1 row.

Dec row K9, k2tog, k12, k2tog tbl, k9.

P 1 row.

Dec row K8, k2tog, k12, k2tog tbl, k8. **30 sts.**

Beg with a p row, work 13 rows in St st.

Shape toes

Dec row K1, [k2tog tbl, k5] 4 times, k1.

P 1 row.

Dec row K1, [k2tog tbl, k4] 4 times, k1.

P 1 row.

Dec row K1, [k2tog tbl, k3] 4 times, k1.

P 1 row.

Dec row K1, [k2tog tbl, k2] 4 times, k1. **14 sts.**

Dec row [P2tog] to end. **7 sts.**

Bind off.

to finish

Sew seam across the toes, then cont to sew seam along center of sole and up the center back, reversing seam on cuff. Turn cuff onto right side.

dufflecoat

sizes and measurements
To fit ages 0–3 (3–6: 6–9: 9–12) months
finished measurements
Chest 19 (20^1/$_2$: 22^1/$_2$: 24)in
Length to shoulder 8^1/$_4$ (9^1/$_2$: 10^1/$_4$: 11)in
Sleeve length (with cuff turned back) 5 (6: 6^3/$_4$: 7^1/$_2$)in

materials
6 (6: 7: 8) x 1^3/$_4$oz/50g balls Debbie Bliss Rialto DK in gray
Pair each of sizes 3 and 6 knitting needles
4 buttons

gauge
22 sts and 48 rows to 4in square over garter st using size 6 needles.

abbreviations
See page 25.

back

With size 6 needles, cast on 53 (57: 63: 67) sts.
Work in garter st (k every row) until back measures 4³/₄ (5¹/₂: 6: 6¹/₄)in from cast-on edge, ending with a wrong-side row.
Shape armholes
Bind off 4 sts at beg of next 2 rows. **45 (49: 55: 59) sts.**
Work even until back measures 8¹/₄ (9¹/₂: 10¹/₄: 11)in from cast-on edge, ending with a wrong-side row.
Shape shoulders
Bind off 11 (12: 14: 15) sts at beg of next 2 rows.
Bind off rem 23 (25: 27: 29) sts.

pocket linings
(make 2)

With size 6 needles, cast on 12 (13: 15: 16) sts.
K 28 (30: 32: 34) rows.
Leave these sts on a holder.

left front

With size 6 needles, cast on 38 (41: 45: 48) sts.
K 27 (29: 31: 33) rows.
Place pocket
Next row (right side) K3, bind off next 12 (13: 15: 16) sts, k to end.
Next row K23 (25: 27: 29), k across sts of first pocket lining, k3.
Cont in garter st until front measures 4³/₄ (5¹/₂: 6: 6¹/₄)in from cast-on edge, ending with a wrong-side row.
Shape armhole
Bind off 4 sts at beg of next row. **34 (37: 41: 44) sts.**
Work even until front measures same as Back to shoulder, ending at armhole edge.
Shape shoulder
Next row Bind off 11 (12: 14: 15) sts, k to end.
K 1 row.
Leave rem 23 (25: 27: 29) sts on a spare needle.

right front

With size 6 needles, cast on 38 (41: 45: 48) sts.
K 27 (29: 31: 33) rows.
Place pocket
Next row K23 (25: 27: 29), bind off next 12 (13: 15: 16) sts, k to end.
Next row K3, k across sts of second pocket lining, k to end.
Cont in garter st until front measures 3 (3¹/₂: 3¹/₂: 3¹/₂)in from cast-on edge, ending with a wrong-side row.
Buttonhole row K3, yo, k2tog, k13 (15: 17: 19), k2tog, yo, k to end.
Cont in garter st until front measures 4³/₄ (5¹/₂: 6: 6¹/₄)in from cast-on edge, ending with a right-side row.

Shape armhole
Bind off 4 sts at beg of next row. **34 (37: 41: 44) sts.**
Work even until front measures 5 (6: 6^1/$_4$: 6^3/$_4$)in from cast-on edge, ending with a wrong-side row.
Buttonhole row K3, yo, k2tog, k13 (15: 17: 19), k2tog, yo, k to end.
Work even until front measures same as Back to shoulder, ending at armhole edge.
Shape shoulder
Next row Bind off 11 (12: 14: 15) sts, k to end. **23 (25: 27: 29) sts.**
Do not break off yarn; leave sts on the needle.

hood

Sew shoulder seams.
Next row (right side) K23 (25: 27: 29) sts from right front, cast on 34 (37: 40: 44) sts, k23 (25: 27: 29) sts from left front. **80 (87: 94: 102) sts.**
Cont in garter st until hood measures 7 (8: 8^1/$_2$: 9^1/$_2$)in, ending with a wrong-side row.
Bind off.

sleeves

With size 6 needles, cast on 29 (31: 33: 35) sts.
K 13 (13: 17: 17) rows.
Change to size 3 needles.
K 12 (12: 16: 16) rows.
Change to size 6 needles.
Inc and work into garter st 1 st at each end of the next row and every foll 8th row until there are 41 (45: 49: 53) sts.
Work even until sleeve measures 6^3/$_4$ (7^1/$_2$: 8^3/$_4$: 9^1/$_2$)in from cast-on edge, ending with a wrong-side row.
Mark each edge of last row with a colored thread.
Work 8 rows more.
Bind off.

to finish

Fold hood in half and sew top seam. Easing in fullness, sew cast-on edge of hood to sts bound off at back neck. Matching center of bound-off edge of sleeve to shoulder, sew sleeves to armholes, stitching row ends above markers to sts bound off at underarm. Sew side and sleeve seams. Sew down pocket linings. Sew on buttons.

changing mat bag

size
15³/₄in by 23¹/₄in

materials
6 x 1³/₄oz/50g balls Debbie Bliss Cotton DK in pale blue
Pair of size 6 knitting needles
Wipe-clean fabric for lining, 17in by 24¹/₂in
3¹/₄yd of tape or ribbon

gauge
20 sts and 32 rows to 4in square over patt using size 6 needles.

abbreviations
See page 25.

to make

With size 6 needles, cast on 75 sts.
1st and 3rd rows (wrong side) Purl.
2nd row K1, *p1, k1; rep from * to end.
4th row P1, *k1, p1; rep from * to end.
These 4 rows form the patt and are repeated throughout.
Cont in patt until work measures 23$\frac{1}{4}$in from cast-on edge, ending with a right-side row.
Bind off knitwise.

pocket

With size 6 needles, cast on 13 sts for pocket bottom.
1st row (right side) K1, *p1, k1; rep from * to end.
2nd and 4th rows Purl.
3rd row P1, *k1, p1; rep from * to end.
These 4 rows form the patt and are repeated.
Work in patt for 1$\frac{1}{2}$in, ending with a p row.
Shape sides
Cast on and take into patt, 9 sts at beg of next 2 rows. **31 sts.**
Cont in patt until pocket measures 6in from side cast-on edges, ending with a right-side row.
Bind off knitwise.

handles (make 2)

With size 6 needles, cast on 9 sts.
Beg with a k row, work 6 rows in St st.
1st inc row K1, M1, k1, [p1, k1] 3 times, M1, k1. **11 sts.**
P 1 row.
2nd inc row K1, M1, k1, [p1, k1] 4 times, M1, k1. **13 sts.**
Place a marker at each end of last row.
1st and 3rd rows Purl.
2nd row K2, [p1, k1] 5 times, k1.
4th row K1, [p1, k1] 6 times.
Rep the last 4 rows until handle measures 10in from cast-on edge, ending with a 4th patt row.
P 1 row.
1st dec row K2tog tbl, p1, [k1, p1] 4 times, k2tog. **11 sts.**
P 1 row.
2nd dec row K2tog tbl, p1, [k1, p1] 3 times, k2tog. **9 sts.**
Place a marker at each end of last row.
Beg with a p row, work 6 rows in St st.
Bind off.

to finish

Sew pocket side cast-on edges to row ends of pocket bottom. Position the pocket on the right side of the mat, 4in down from bound-off edge and 4in in from right-hand side edge, and slip stitch in place. Fold each handle in half and sew together row ends to form seam between markers. Position handles on the short ends of the mat, and sew the St st sections to the mat. Cut ribbon/tape into 8 pieces and sew to long edges of the mat, so they will tie at the sides when the mat is folded in half. Fold $\frac{5}{8}$in of lining fabric to wrong side around all edges, and place on the wrong side of the mat. Slip stitch around all edges, so hiding handle ends and raw ends of ribbon/tape.

yarndistributors

For suppliers of Debbie Bliss yarns please contact:

USA
Knitting Fever Inc.
315 Bayview Avenue
Amityville
NY 11701
USA
t: +1 516 546 3600
f: +1 516 546 6871
e: admin@knittingfever.com
w: www.knittingfever.com

CANADA
Diamond Yarns Ltd.
155 Martin Ross Avenue
Unit 3
Toronto
Ontario M3J 2L9
Canada
t: +1 416 736 6111
f: +1 416 736 6112
w. www.diamondyarn.com

UK & WORLDWIDE DISTRIBUTORS
Designer Yarns Ltd.
Units 8–10
Newbridge Industrial Estate
Pitt Street
Keighley
West Yorkshire BD21 4PQ
UK
t: +44 (0) 1535 664222
f: +44 (0) 1535 664333
e: david@designeryarns.uk.com
w. www.designeryarns.uk.com

BELGIUM/HOLLAND
Pavan
Meerlaanstraat 73
9860 Balegem (Oostrezele)
Belgium
t: +32 (0) 9 221 85 94
f: +32 (0) 9 221 56 62
e: pavan@pandora.be

DENMARK
Fancy Knit
Hovedvejen 71
8586 Oerum Djurs
Ramten
Denmark
t: +45 59 46 21 89
f: +45 59 46 8018
e: roenneburg@mail.dk

FINLAND
Handicraft House PRIIMA
Käsityötalo
Hämeentie 26
00530 Helsinki
Finland
t: +358 (0) 9 753 1716
f: +358 (0) 9 7318 0009
e: info@priima.net
w: www.priima.net

FRANCE
Elle Tricote
8 Rue du Coq
La Petite France
67000 Strasbourg
France
t: +33 (0) 388 230313
f: +33 (0) 8823 0169
w: www.elletricote.com

GERMANY/AUSTRIA/
SWITZERLAND
Designer Yarns
Handelsagentur Klaus Koch
Sachsstraße 30
D-50259 Pulheim-Brauweiler
Germany
t: +49 (0) 2234 205453
f: +49 (0) 2234 205456
e: kk@designeryarns.de
w: www.designeryarns.de

ICELAND
Storkurinn
Langavegi 59
101 Reykjavík
Iceland
t: +354 551 8258
f: +354 562 8252

SPAIN
Oyambre Needlework SL
Balmes, 200 At.4
08006 Barcelona
Spain
t: +34 (0)93 487 26 72
f: +34 (0)93 218 6694/368 3480
e: info@oyambreonline.com

SWEDEN
Nysta garn och textil
Luntmakargatan 50
S-113 58 Stockholm
Sweden
t: +46 (0)8 612 0330
e: info@nysta.se
w: www.nysta.se

AUSTRALIA/NEW ZEALAND
Prestige Yarns Pty Ltd.
PO Box 39
Bulli
NSW 2516
Australia
t: +61 (0) 2 4285 6669
e: info@prestigeyarns.com
w: www.prestigeyarns.com

JAPAN
Hobbyra Hobbyre
5-23-37 Higashi-Ohi
Shinagawa-ku
Tokyo 140-0011
Japan
t: +81 3 3472 1104
f: +81 3 3472 1196
w: www.hobbyra-hobbyre.com

MEXICO
Estambres Crochet SA de CV
Aaron Saenz 1891–7
Col. Santa Maria
Monterrey
N.L. 64650
Mexico
t: +52 (81) 8335 3870
e: abremer@redmundial.com.mx

For more information on my other books and yarns, please visit www.debbieblissonline.com

glossary of patterns

hooded carrying bag pages 56–59

baby aged (months)	0–3	3–6	
back length	21¾	23½	in

lacy shawl pages 60–63

length	43in
width	37in

toy lamb pages 64–67

height	4in
length	5½in

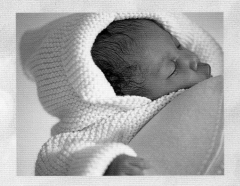

141

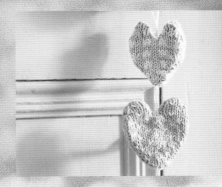

romper panties pages 70–73

baby aged (months)	3–6	6–9	
finished hips	20	22	in
length	8¾	9½	in

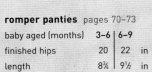

baby shorts pages 74–77

baby aged (months)	3–6	6–9	
finished hips	20	22	in
length	10¾	11¾	in

heart mobile pages 78–81

size	small	medium	large	
length	3¼	3½	4	in

bathrobe pages 82–87

baby aged (months)	6	12	18	24	
finished chest	23¼	24¾	26½	28	in
back length	16½	19	21¼	23½	in
sleeve length	6¼	7	8¼	9½	in

vest pages 88–93

baby aged (months)	0–3	3–6	6–9	9–12	
finished chest	17¾	19¾	21	22¾	in
back length	8¼	9½	10¼	11	in

pinafore dress pages 94–97

baby aged (months)	3–6	6–9	9–12	
finished chest	18½	20½	22½	in
back length	14½	16½	19	in

baby beanbag pages 98–99

length	27½in
width	27½in

felted slippers pages 100–103

baby aged (months)	0–3

reversible hat pages 106–109

baby aged (months)	3–6	9–12

classic cardigan pages 110–115

baby aged (months)	0–3	3–6	6–9	9–12	
finished chest	16½	18	19¾	21¼	in
back length	7¾	8¾	9¾	11	in
sleeve length	4¾	5½	6¼	7	in

stroller blanket pages 116–121

length	28in
width	17¾in

shawl collar sweater pages 122–125

baby aged (months)	3–6	6–9	9–12	12–18	18–24	
finished chest	19¾	20¾	23½	24¾	27½	in
back length	9½	10¼	11½	12½	14¼	in
sleeve length	5½	6¼	7	8	8¾	in

143

cable socks pages 126–129

baby aged (months)	3–6

duffle coat pages 130–135

baby aged (months)	0–3	3–6	6–9	9–12	
finished chest	19	20½	22½	24	in
back length	8¼	9½	10¼	11	in
sleeve length	5	6	6¾	7½	in

changing mat bag pages 136–138

length	23¼in
width	15¾in

Dedication

to my own essential family

For a complete list of Debbie Bliss titles and other knitting books, contact:

Trafalgar Square Books

388 Howe Hill Road

North Pomfret, Vermont 05053

800.423.4525

www.trafalgarbooks.com

acknowledgments

This book would not have been possible without the contribution of the following:

Jane O'Shea, **Lisa Pendreigh,** and **Mary Evans** at Quadrille Publishing who have been such an inspirational team to work with.

Julie Mansfield, the stylist, whose input, as always, has been invaluable.

Debi Treloar, for the simply beautiful photographs, and her assistant Ciara.

Sally Kvalheim, who did such a great job baby grooming.

And, of course, the fantastic mothers and babies: **Casey** and **Evelyn**, **Charlie, Dylan, Funsho** and **Levi, Grace, Guy, Hayden, Jake, Katherine, Kristina, Luca, Mathilda, Noah**, **Rachel** and **Joshua, Rosie,** and **Sydney**.

Rosy Tucker, for pattern checking and creative as well as practial support.

Penny Hill, for her essential pattern compiling and organizing the knitters.

The knitters, for the huge effort they put into creating perfectly knitted garments under deadline pressure: **Cynthia Brent, Barbara Clapham, Pat Church, Pat Clack, Jacqui Dunt, Shirley Kennet, Maisie Lawrence,** and **Frances Wallace**.

My fantastic agent, **Heather Jeeves**.

The distributors, agents, retailers, and **knitters** who support all my books and yarns, and make all my projects possible.